AF477598

Morten Buch

The Last Resort
Letzte Zuflucht

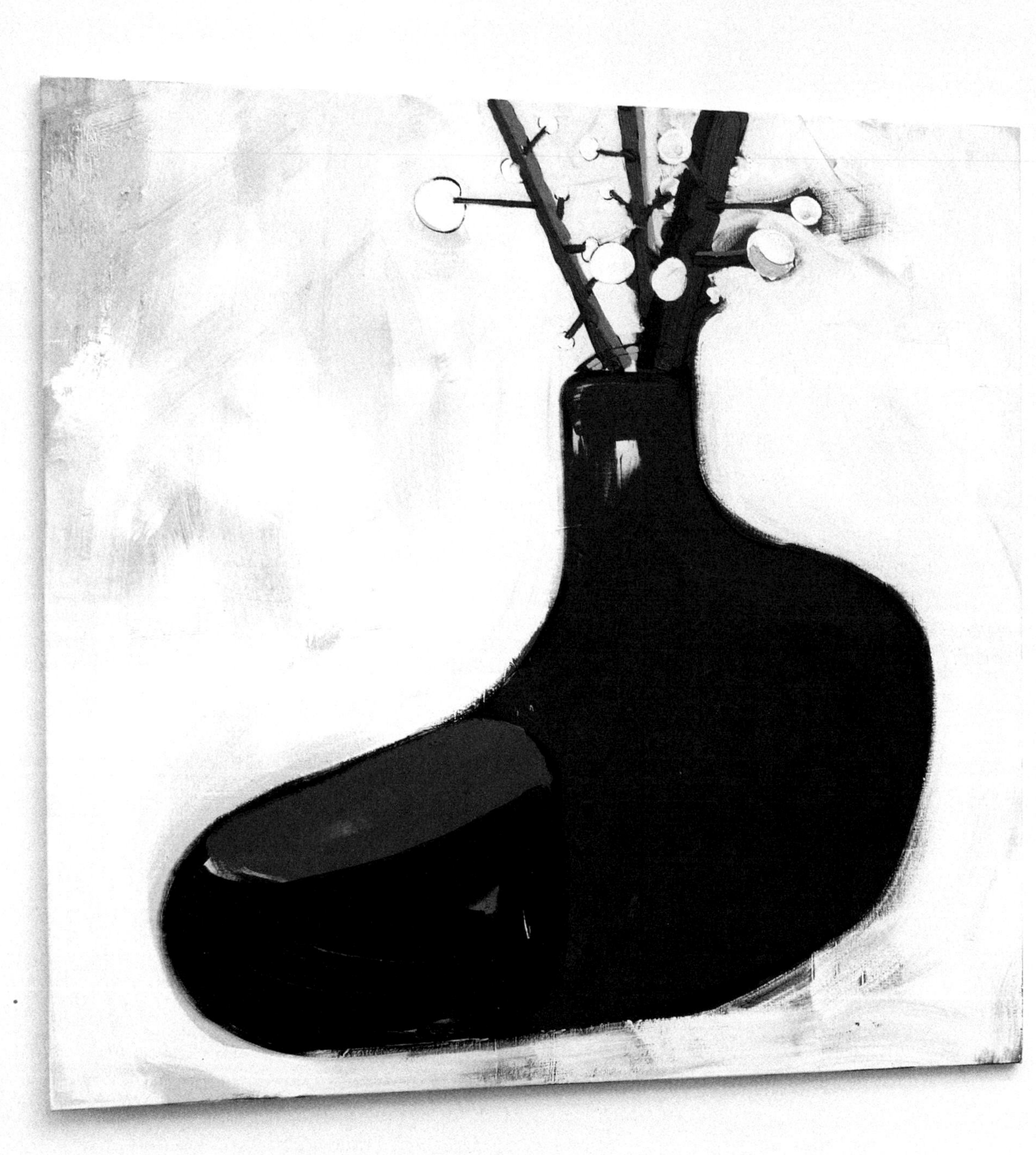

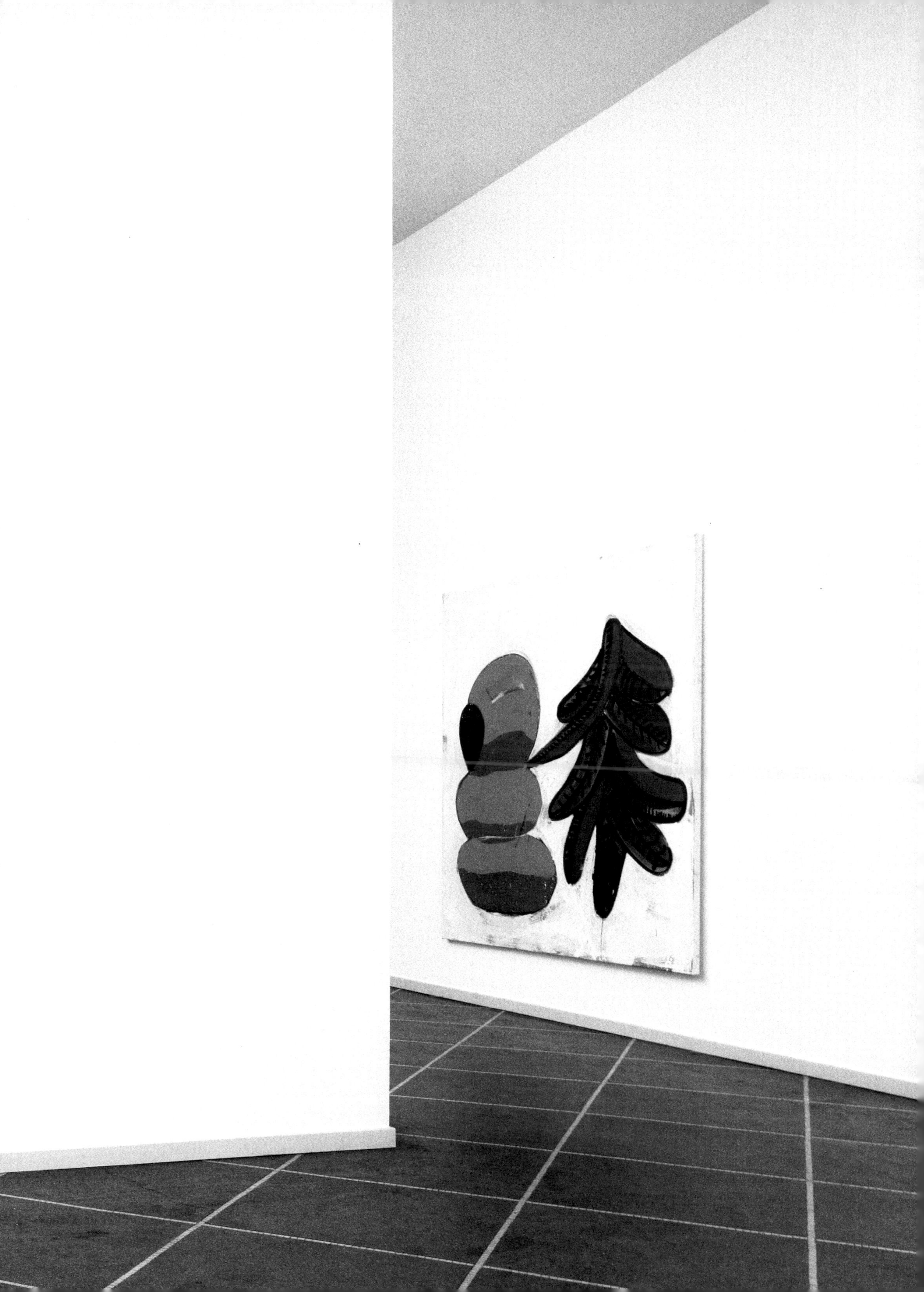

# Morten

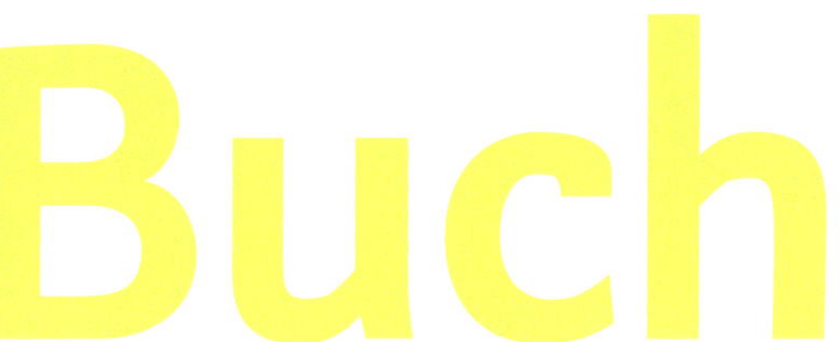


# The Last Resort   Letzte Zuflucht

herausgegeben von | edited by   VIOLA WEIGEL

mit Beiträgen von
with contributions from   VIOLA WEIGEL
CLAUS HAGEDORN-OLSEN
MAIBRITT PEDERSEN

KUNSTHALLE WILHELMSHAVEN   KERBER EDITION YOUNG ART

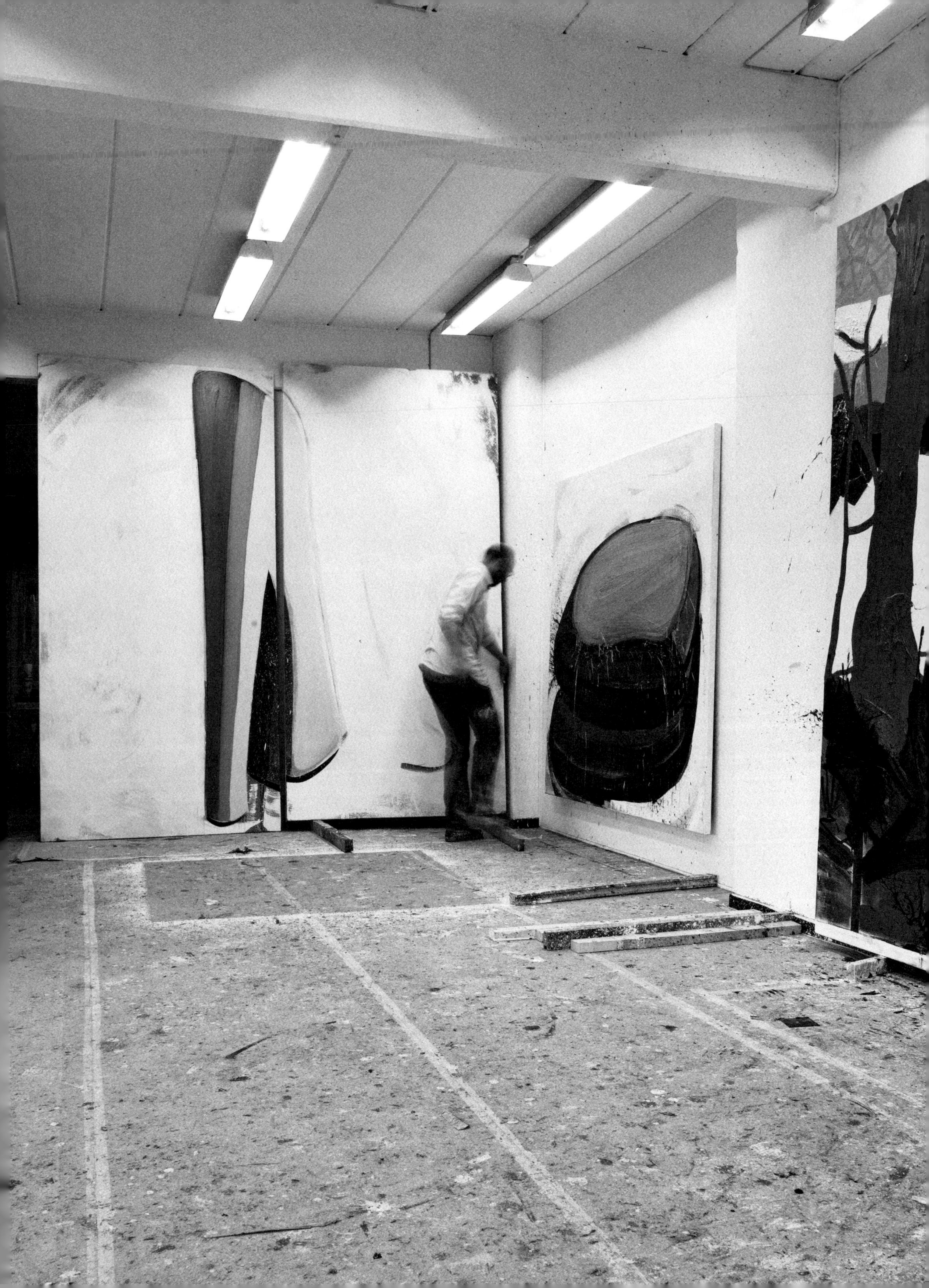

# Inhalt | Contents

# Vorwort

Ist die Abbildung der Wirklichkeit die letzte Bastion in der Gegenwartskunst geworden, um mit der Malerei über andere Bildmedien zu triumphieren? Der Avantgarde bot die Gattung der Dingdarstellung – das Stillleben – bereits um 1900 ein besonders fruchtbares Experimentierfeld, um neue Techniken und Darstellungsformen zu erproben. Gottfried Boehms nachdrückliche Forderung, durch die „Aktualität der Bilder" und die „steigende Medienflut" nicht die grundlegenden Probleme des „Bildes" aus dem Auge zu verlieren, erscheint nicht überholt und zeitgenössische Künstler besonders zu beschäftigen (vgl. *Was ist ein Bild?*, München 1994). Denn ein Jahrhundert später ist das wohlbekannte Triumvirat der Kunstgattungen – Stillleben, Figurenbild und Landschaft – in der Gegenwartskunst wieder unübersehbar zurück. Von dem vielzitierten „Hunger nach (figurativen) Bildern" in den 80er-Jahren kann in diesem Fall aber keine Rede sein. Denn die vermeintlich traditionelle Ordnung des Bildes wird vielmehr zum anspruchsvollen Konzept, um die zukünftige Richtung der Kunst und damit das Potenzial eines „Bildes" vom vertrauten Terrain aus zu erforschen.

Morten Buch, geboren 1970 in Kopenhagen, stellt eine markante Persönlichkeit in der dänischen Kunst dar. Sein vielseitiges Œuvre erschwert eine einfache Einordnung – doch bestehen enge Bezüge zu Künstlern, wie Troels Wörsel, Erik A. Frandsen, Lars Nørgård oder Tal R, die eine Art methodische Inventur der Moderne mit ihren neo-expressionistischen, neo-primitiven und figurativen Wurzeln betreiben. Buchs Werkgruppe mit circa 20 Ölgemälden aus dem Jahr 2006 entfesselte unser besonderes Interesse und war ausschlaggebend für die Realisierung dieser Ausstellung. Präzise umrissene Darstellungen von Vasen, Schuhen, Zelten oder Matratzen auf großen Leinwänden konfrontieren uns mit raumgreifender, ja: physischer, Präsenz. Die jeweilige Form- und Farbgestaltung verleihen dem Ding eine paradoxe Wirkung, eine „vertraute Fremdheit" (Morten Buch), die sich nicht zwischen anziehender Schönheit und kühler Abweisung entscheiden kann: Es entsteht ein Fest sinnbetonter Malerei, die uns überrollt, einlullt und doch irritiert zurücklässt. Denn die dargestellten, vermeintlich vertrauten Dinge lösen sich durch ihre bis auf 300 × 300 cm überzeichneten Formate vom gewohnten Idealbild und erscheinen uns fremd; so fremd wie die bizarren Manipulationen in heutiger Digitalbildkultur. Buchs „mögliche" Räume schreiben nicht eigentlich die gegenständliche Kunst fort, sondern vielmehr eine Form der Abstraktion zwischen Pop-Art und Farbfeldmalerei, die mit der Spannung von Wahrnehmung, Bildkörper und Haptik umgeht und dabei den Betrachter zwingt, die Wirklichkeit aus einer ganz anderen Perspektive wahrzunehmen.

Aktuelle Ausstellungen über Vertreter der Neuen Figuration wie Georg Baselitz, Markus Lüpertz oder Dieter Krieg lenken wieder den Blick auf eine Malerei, die in den 80er-Jahren

# Preface

Has the depiction of reality become the last bastion of contemporary art whereby painting will triumph over other visual media? Around 1900 the Avant-garde movement was already rendering the genre given over to the representation of things – the still life – especially fertile ground on which to experiment with new techniques and forms of representation. Gottfried Boehm's emphatic appeal that the fundamental questions relating to the "image" not be lost sight of as a result of the "actuality of the image" and the "increasing barrage of mass media" appears to remain relevant today and to be a particular preoccupation of contemporary artists (*Was ist ein Bild?*, München 1994). A century later the return to contemporary art of the familiar triumvirate of artistic genres – still life, figure and landscape painting – is unmistakable. In this instance, however, there can be no question of the much-cited "hunger for (figurative) images" of the 1980s since the supposedly traditional order of the image is in fact becoming an elaborate strategy with which to explore the future direction of art, and thereby also to explore the potential of an "image" in a departure from familiar territory.

Morten Buch, born in 1970 in Copenhagen, presents a striking personality in Danish art. The diversity of his œuvre makes it difficult to categorise – nevertheless, there are strong connections with the work of artists such as Troels Wörsel, Erik A. Frandsen, Lars Nørgård and Tal R, who pursue something like a methodical inventory of modern art with their neo-expressionist, neo-primitive and figurative roots. Buch's collection of around 20 oil paintings from 2006 captured our particular interest and was decisive in the realisation of this exhibition. Clearly outlined representations of vases, shoes, tents and mattresses on large canvases confront us with a tangible, indeed physical, presence. The given form and colouring of the thing give rise to a paradoxical effect, a "familiar strangeness" (Morten Buch), that sits irresolutely between the alluringly attractive and the forcefully repellent. The result is a feat of sensuous paintings that overwhelm us, lull us and yet still leave us bemused: their exaggerated formats of up to 300 × 300 cm render the portrayed and supposedly familiar things divorced from their familiar and quintessential form and they appear alien to us; as alien as the bizarre manipulations we see in today's culture of digital imagery. Buch's "potential" spaces do not, strictly speaking, perpetuate representational art, but rather a form of abstraction somewhere between Pop art and Colour Field painting that deals with the tension between perception, the body of the image and the haptic, and thereby forces the observer to perceive reality from an entirely different perspective.

Current exhibitions on early representatives of the New Figuration, such as Georg Baselitz, Markus Lüpertz and Dieter Krieg, highlight once again a mode of painting that in

eine neue Welle malerischer Erfindungen in Gang setzte. Vor dem Hintergrund des „Remix" gestischer Malerei eignet sich Buchs Ansatz dafür, um gleichermaßen den Folgen und Möglichkeiten figurativer Malerei aus der Perspektive der skandinavischen Gegenwartskunst, die oft zu rasch mit den deutschen Neuen Wilden der 8oer-Jahre verknüpft wird, nachzuspüren.

Es war eine glückliche Fügung, dass unsere beiden Häuser für diese Kooperation zusammenfanden. Eine ausschlaggebende Rolle spielte dabei Susanne Ottesen von der gleichnamigen Kopenhagener Galerie, der ich meine Ausstellungsidee vorstellte, und die gleich den Kontakt mit Claus Hagedorn-Olsen, dem Direktor des Horsens Kunstmuseum, herstellte. Gleichzeitig war es für uns der richtige Zeitpunkt, sich intensiver mit dem Werk von Morten Buch auseinanderzusetzen. In der Kunsthalle Wilhelmshaven beschäftigen wir uns seit 2007 mit übergreifenden Fragestellungen der Gegenwartskunst, dem ästhetischen Dialog zwischen Architektur und Skulptur (Gereon Krebber), dem Verhältnis von Ökonomie und Visualität (Harald Braun), und im Rahmen von Morten Buch mit der in Wissenschaft und Kunst gleichermaßen aktuellen Diskussion über die Bedeutung der „Dinge". Das Horsens Kunstmuseum wiederum baut seit Mitte der 8oer-Jahre eine bedeutende Sammlung dänischer Gegenwartskunst auf, die sich mit neuen und anderen Wegen der Wirklichkeitsdarstellung befasst. Die Auswahl der Künstler richtet sich danach aus, ob sie zum Nachdenken anregen und nicht einfach nur unterhalten. Seit 2006 zählen auch zwei Gemälde von Morten Buch zur Museumssammlung.

Unser beider herzlicher und großer Dank gilt Morten Buch und seiner Bereitschaft, mit uns seine erste große Einzelausstellung außerhalb Dänemarks vorzubereiten. Herzlich danken möchten wir Susanne Ottesen und ihrem engagierten Galerieteam für ihre wertvolle Unterstützung in allen Fragen. Den Mitarbeitern und Mitarbeiterinnen des Kerber Verlags, Bielefeld, und dem Grafiker Andreas Koch danken wir für die gute Zusammenarbeit bei der Produktion des Katalogbuchs. Der Online-Ausgabe der Internetzeitschrift *www.Kopenhagen.dk* danken wir für die freundliche Genehmigung des Abdrucks des Interviews. Großzügig haben der Statens Kunstfond, Kopenhagen, und dänische Privatsammler unser Ausstellungsprojekt unterstützt. Ohne die substanziellen Beiträge unserer Sponsoren hätten wir aber sowohl die landesübergreifende Ausstellung wie Katalog nicht meistern können. Dem Land Niedersachsen, der Niedersächsischen Lottostiftung, der Sparkasse Wilhelmshaven, der Kulturstiftung der Öffentlichen Versicherungen, Oldenburg, Lantmännen Unibake A/S, HAY, BS Studio A/S, Bestseller A/S, Løvbjerg Fonden A/S, Horsens Kommune, Qurios, VIA University College, Regionshospitalet Horsens, Brædstrup og Odder, Østjydsk Bank A/S, Foreningen Energi Horsens und nicht zuletzt dem Danish Arts Council sei für ihre Unterstützung ganz herzlich gedankt.

Unser Ziel ist es, den Kulturdialog zu vertiefen und damit einen weiteren Brückenschlag zwischen Deutschland und Dänemark in der gemeinsamen Region Nordwest zu verwirklichen. Deshalb sehen wir einer weiteren Zusammenarbeit erwartungsvoll entgegen.

CLAUS HAGEDORN-OLSEN
Direktor Horsens Kunstmuseum

VIOLA WEIGEL
Direktorin Kunsthalle Wilhelmshaven

the 1980s had initiated a new wave of possibilities in painting. Against the backdrop of the gestural painting "Remix", Buch's approach lends itself to pursue, in a similar fashion, the implications and possibilities of figurative painting from the perspective of Scandinavian art, which frequently is all too hastily associated with the German "Neuen Wilden" ("New Wild Ones") of the 1980s.

It was a stroke of good fortune that our two establishments joined forces to collaborate on this project. Instrumental in this was Susanne Ottesen from the Copenhagen art gallery of the same name to whom I presented my idea for an exhibition and who then immediately put us in touch with Claus Hagedorn-Olsen, the director of Horsens Kunstmuseum. Coincidentally, it was the right time for both of us to engage more intensively with Morten Buch's work. Since 2007, Kunsthalle Wilhelmshaven has been engaging with a broad range of issues in contemporary art: with the aesthetic dialogue between architecture and sculpture (Gereon Krebber), the relationship between economy and visuality (Harald Braun) and, in the context of Morten Buch's work, with the debate, equally topical in both science and art, on the significance of "things". Horsens Kunstmuseum, in turn, has, since the middle of the 1980s, been acquiring a major collection of Danish contemporary art that considers new and different approaches to the representation of reality. Artists are chosen on the basis that their work gives cause for reflection and does not merely entertain. Since 2006, two paintings by Morten Buch have also been part of the collection.

We are immensely grateful to Morten Buch and his willingness to work with us on his first major solo exhibition outside Denmark. Many thanks to Susanne Ottesen and her committed team at the gallery for their valuable support in all matters. We extend our grateful appreciation for their cooperation and support in the production of the exhibition catalogue to all employees at Kerber Verlag, Bielefeld and to the graphic designer Andreas Koch. Our thanks go to the online magazine at *www.Kopenhagen.dk* for their kind permission to reproduce the interview. This project received generous backing from the Statens Kunstfond, Copenhagen and from private collectors in Denmark. Without the substantial contributions made by our sponsors, however, neither the transnational exhibition nor the catalogue would have been possible. Sincere thanks also go to Land Niedersachsen, the Niedersächsische Lottostiftung, Sparkasse Wilhelmshaven, the Kulturstiftung der Öffentlichen Versicherungen, Oldenburg, Lantmännen Unibake A/S, HAY, BS Studio A/S, Bestseller A/S, Løvbjerg Fonden A/S, Horsens Kommune, Qurios, VIA University College, Regionshospitalet Horsens, Brædstrup og Odder, Østjydsk Bank A/S, Foreningen Energi Horsens and, not least, the Danish Arts Council.

It is our aim to consolidate this cultural dialogue and thereby establish further links between Germany and Denmark in the collective northwest. We hope therefore to be able to look forward to further collaboration in the future.

Claus Hagedorn  
Director Horsens Kunstmuseum

Viola Weigel  
Director Kunsthalle Wilhelmshaven

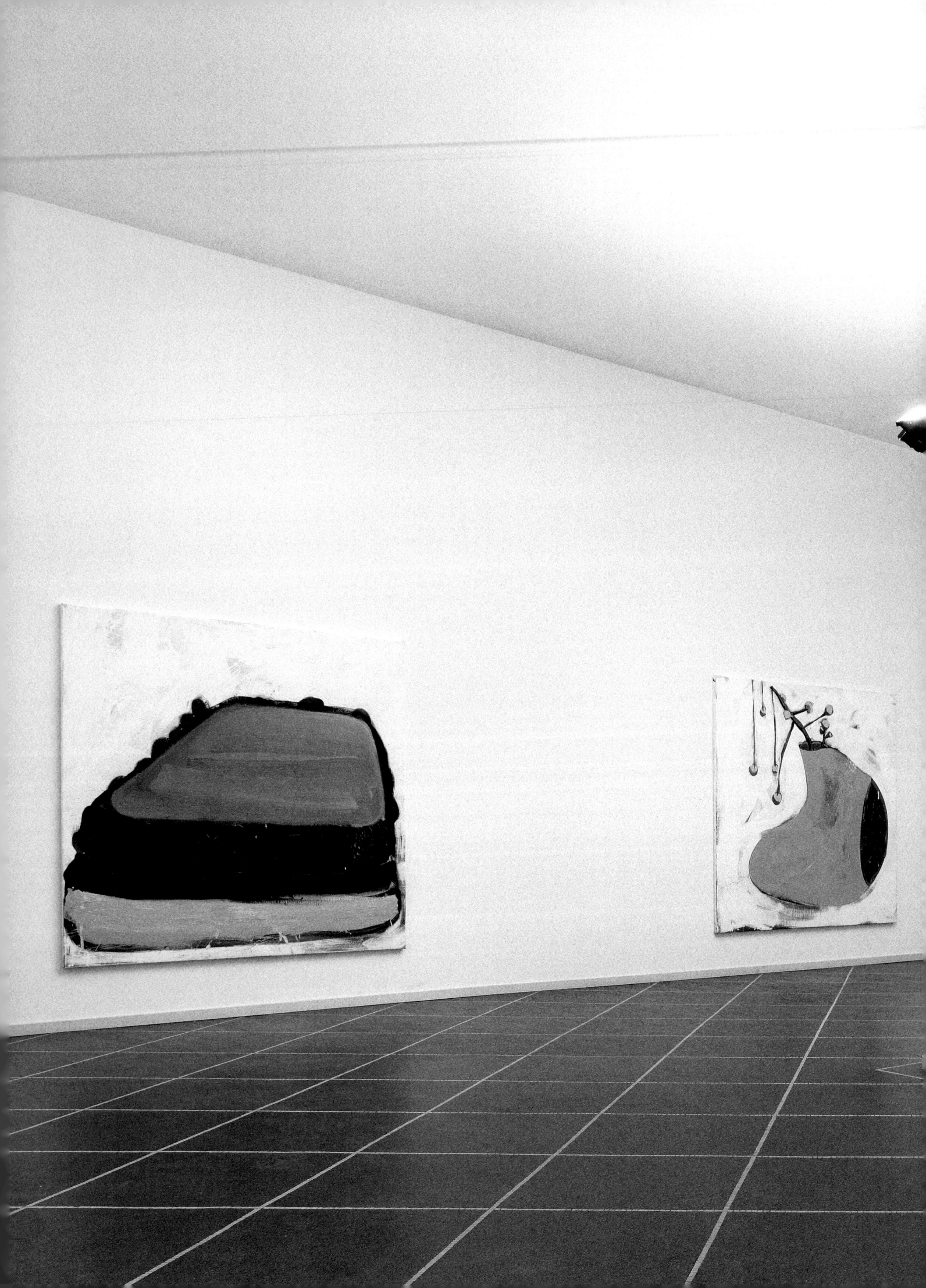

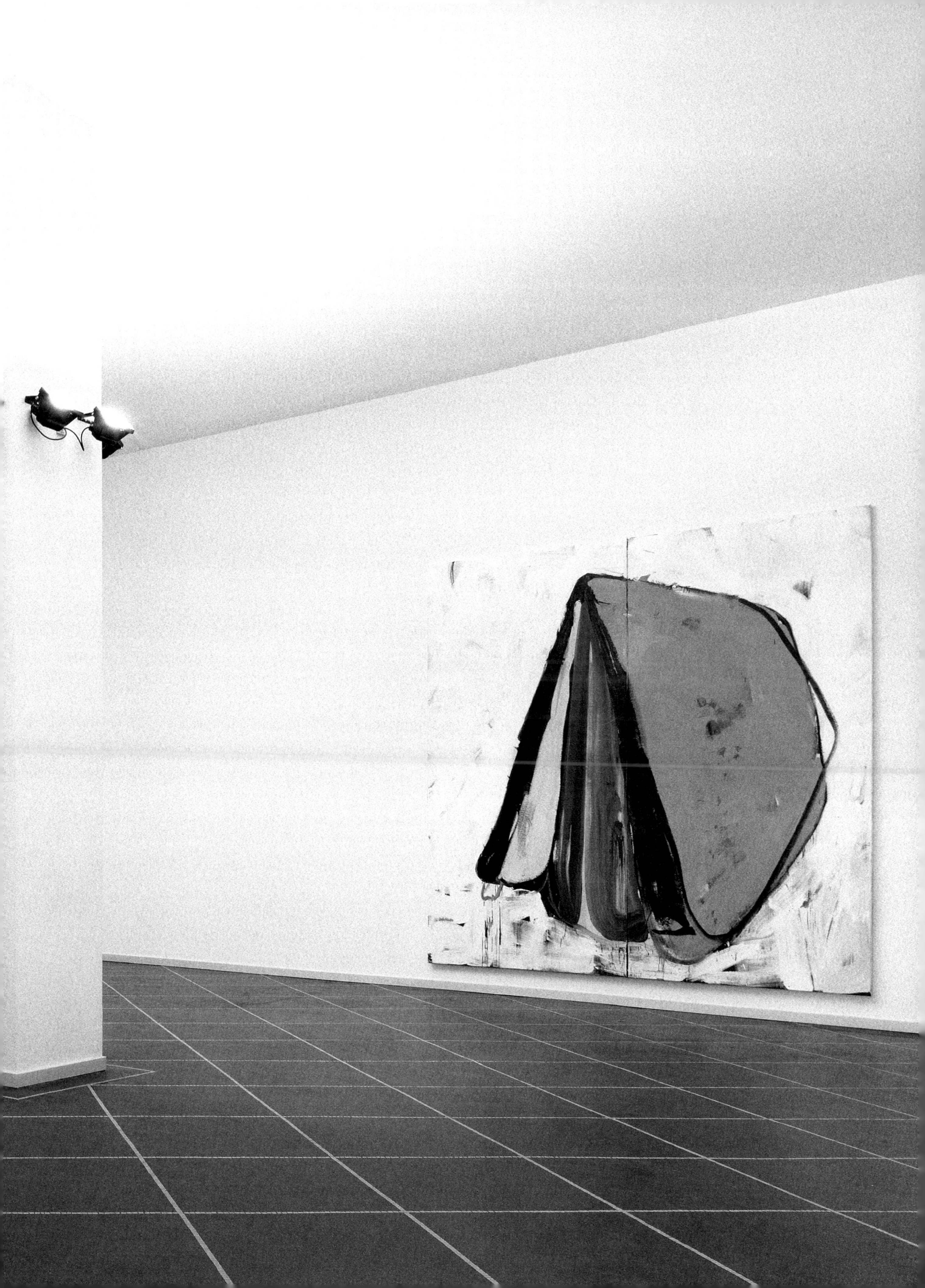

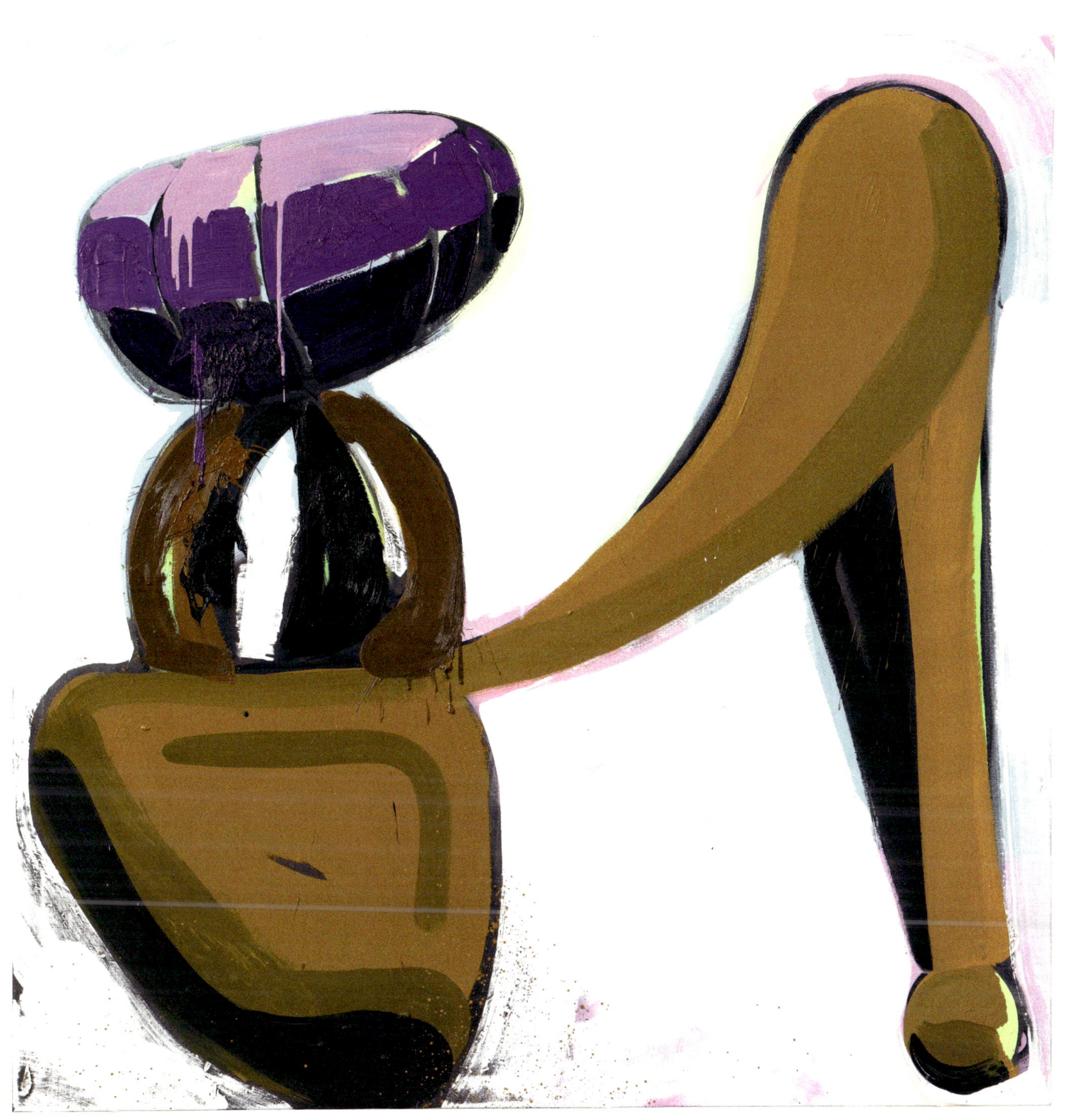



Sko 2006

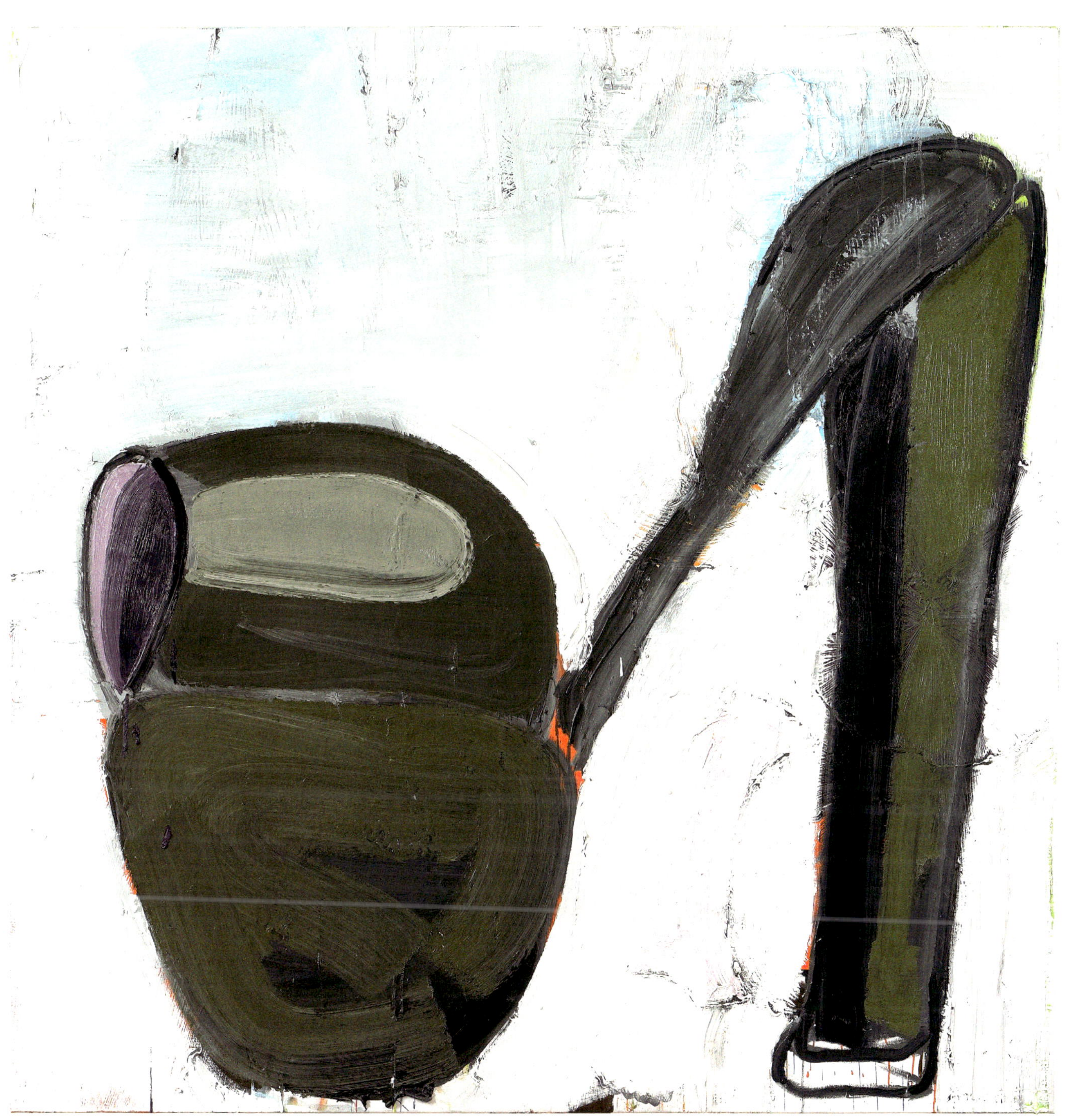

Sko 2006

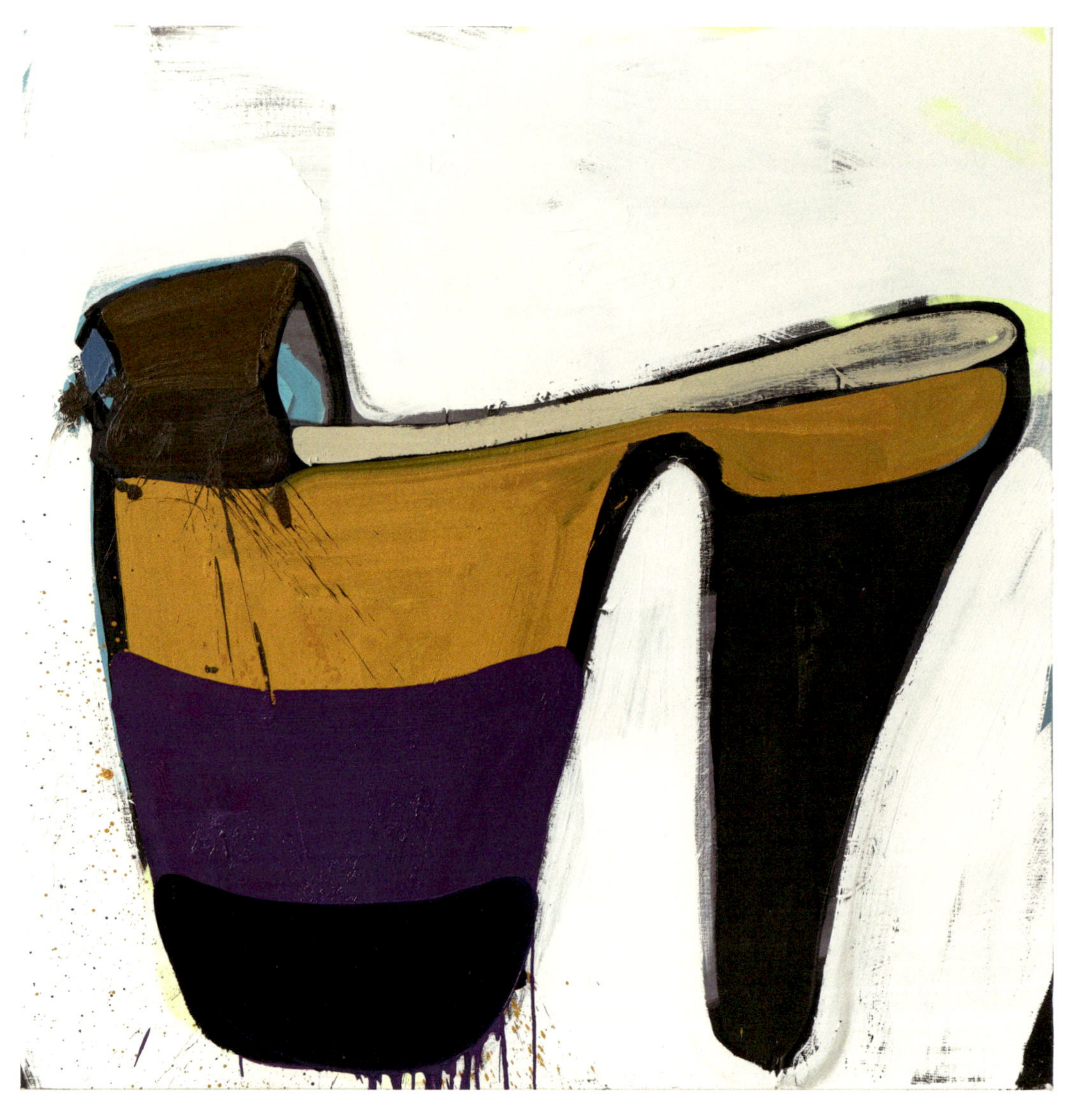

**Sko** 2006

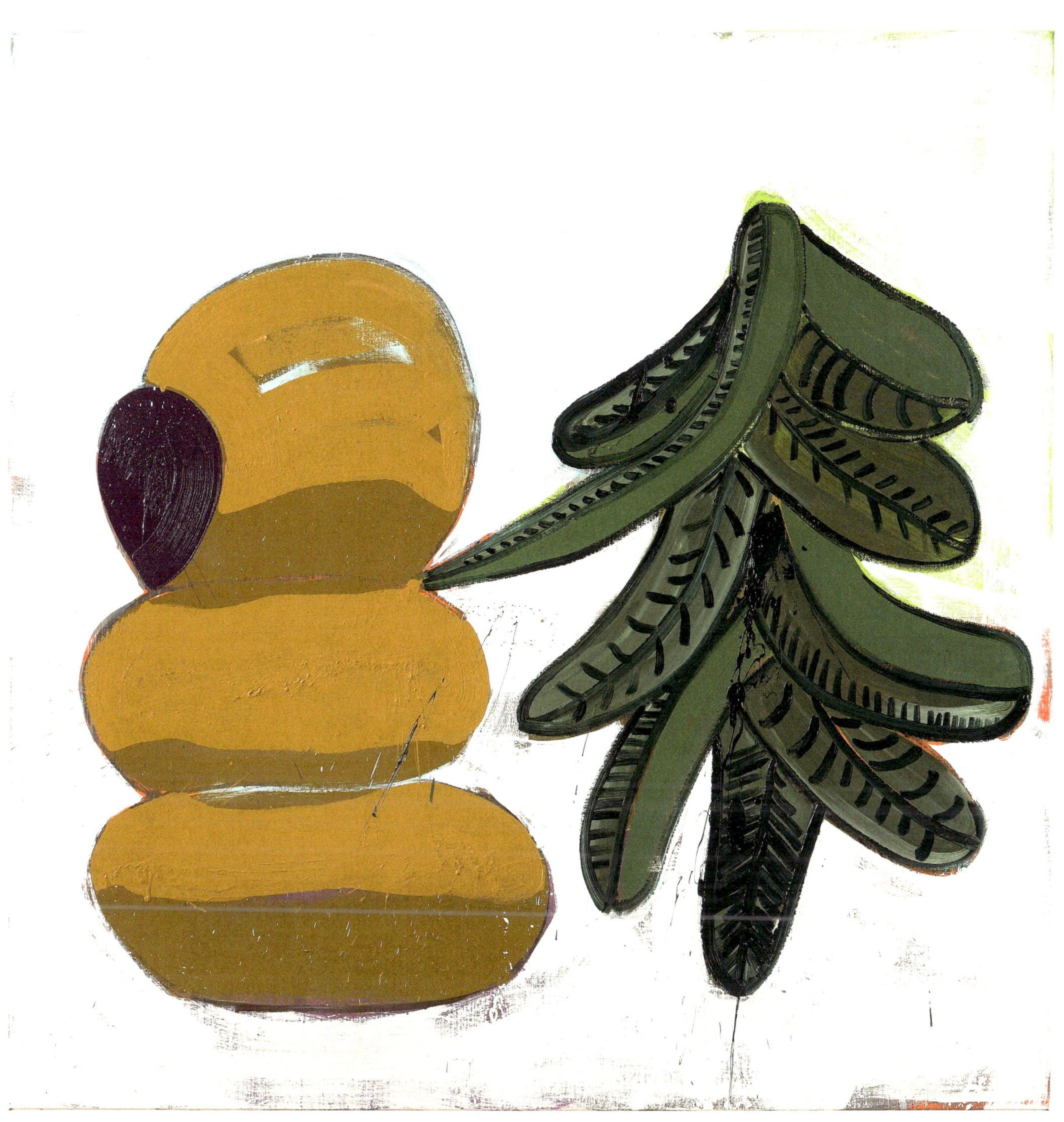

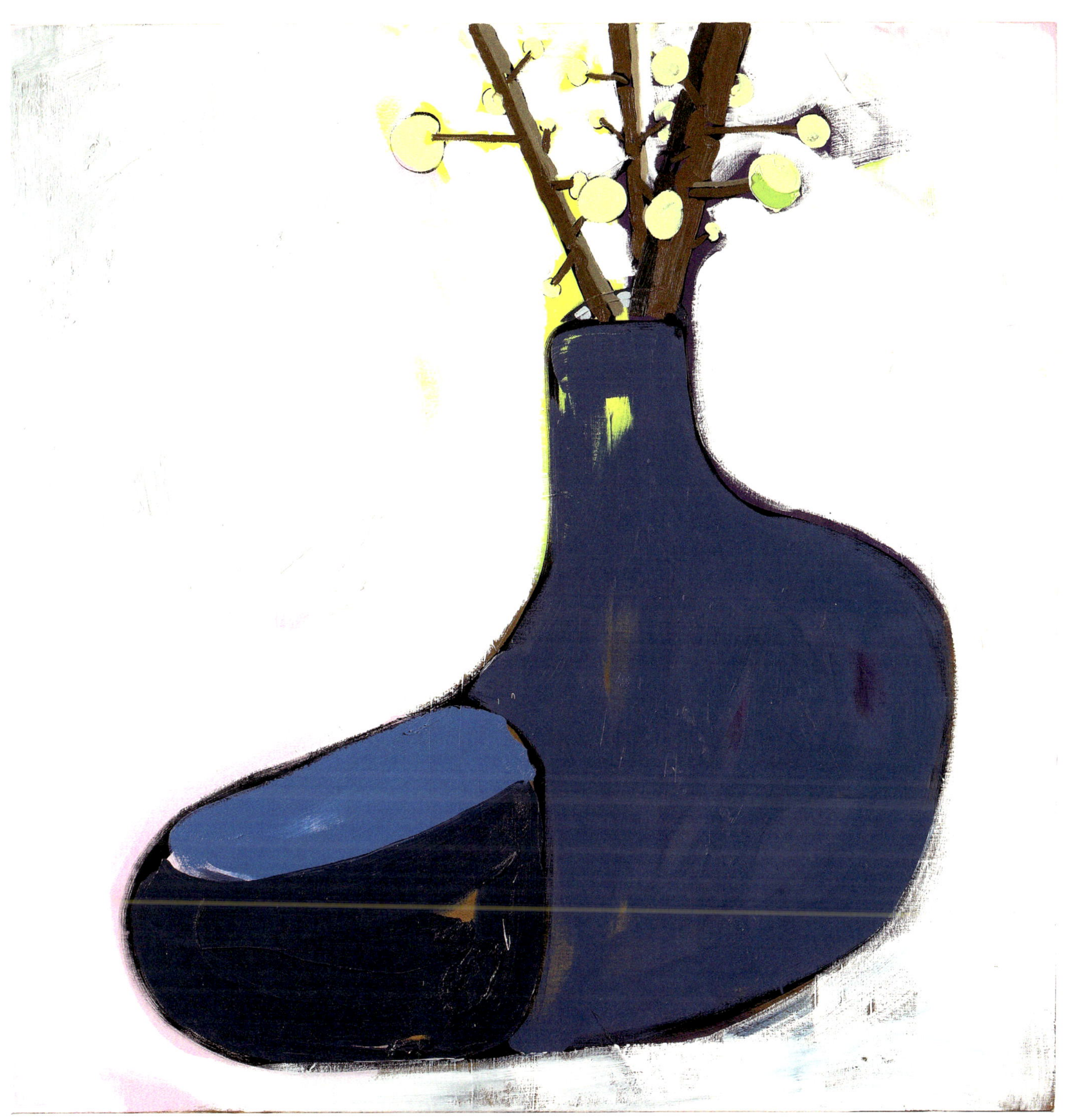

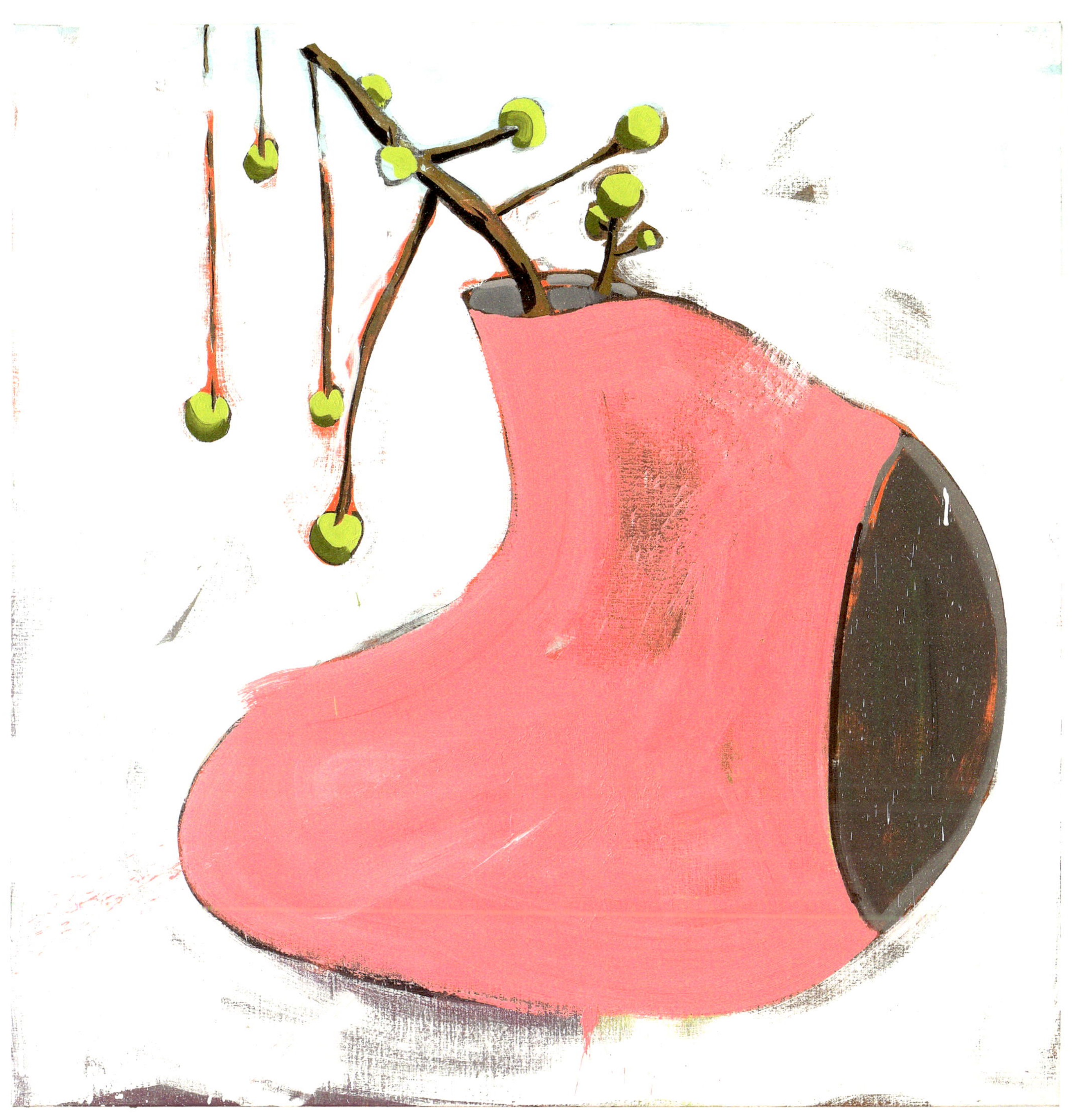

Vase 2006

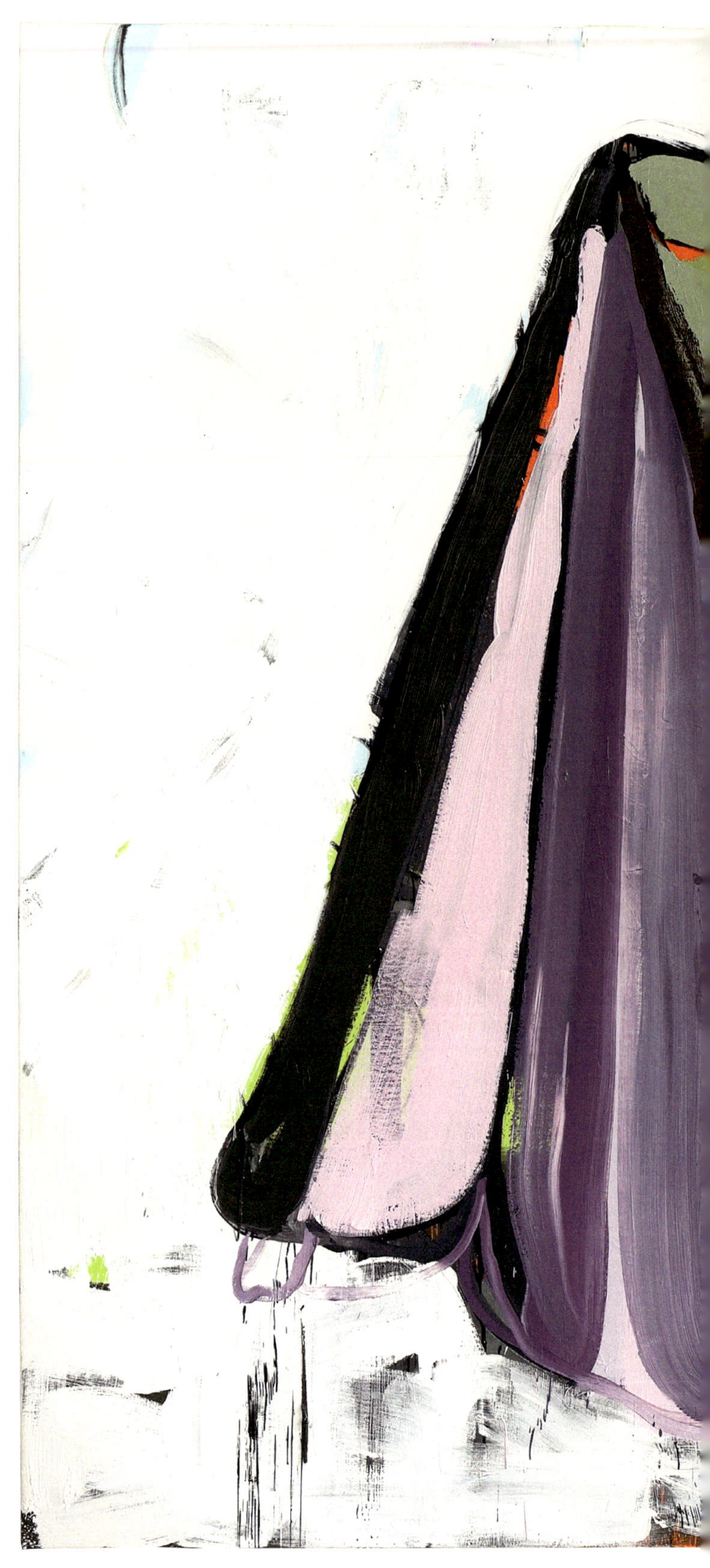

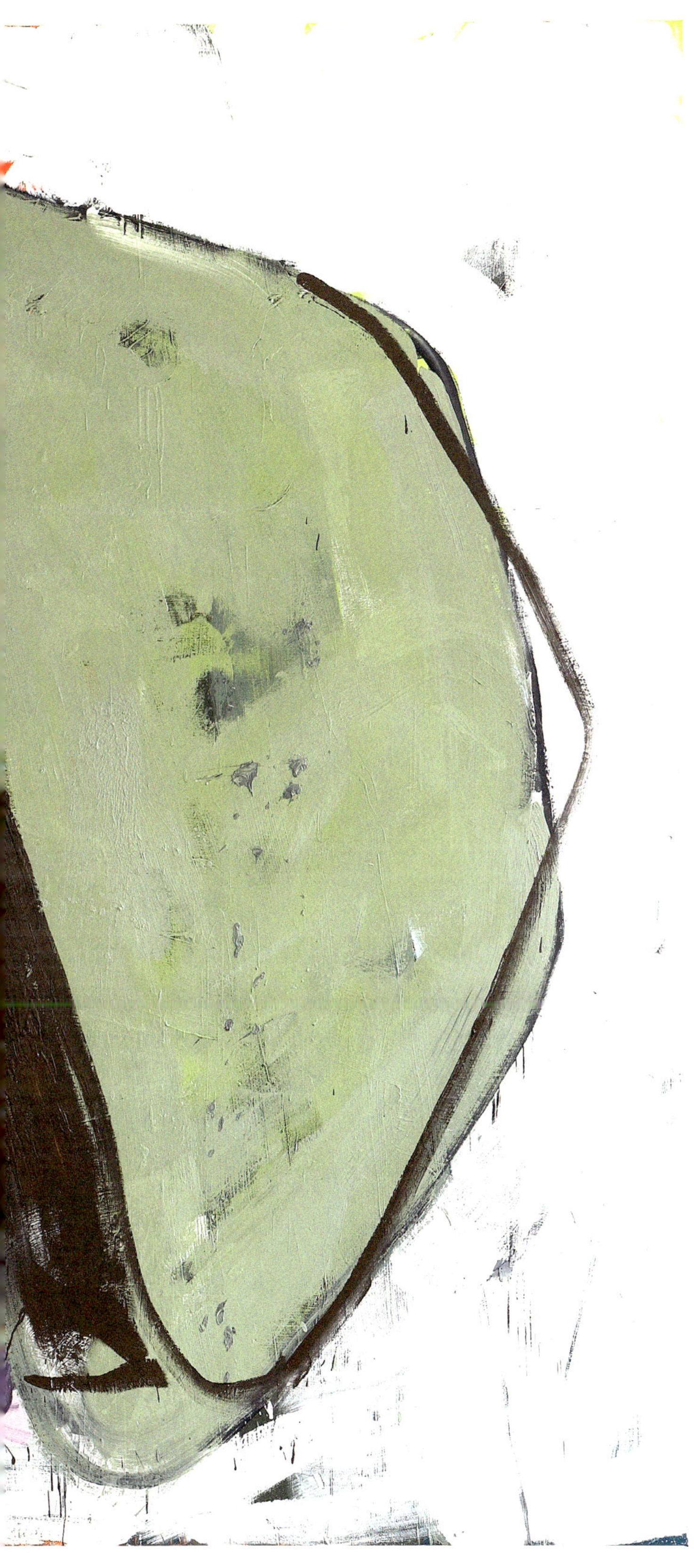

Telt 2006

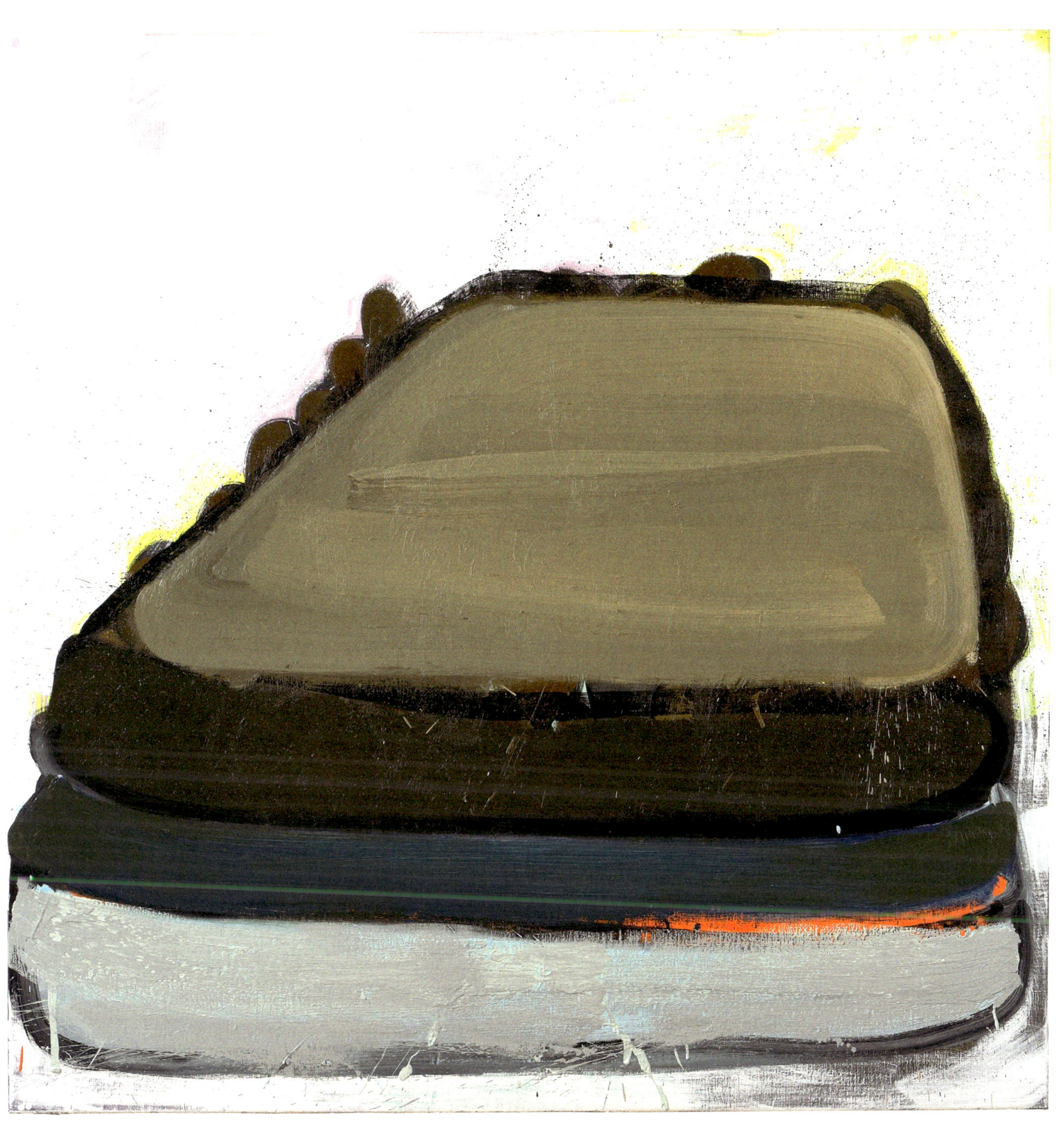

Dobbeltmadras 2006

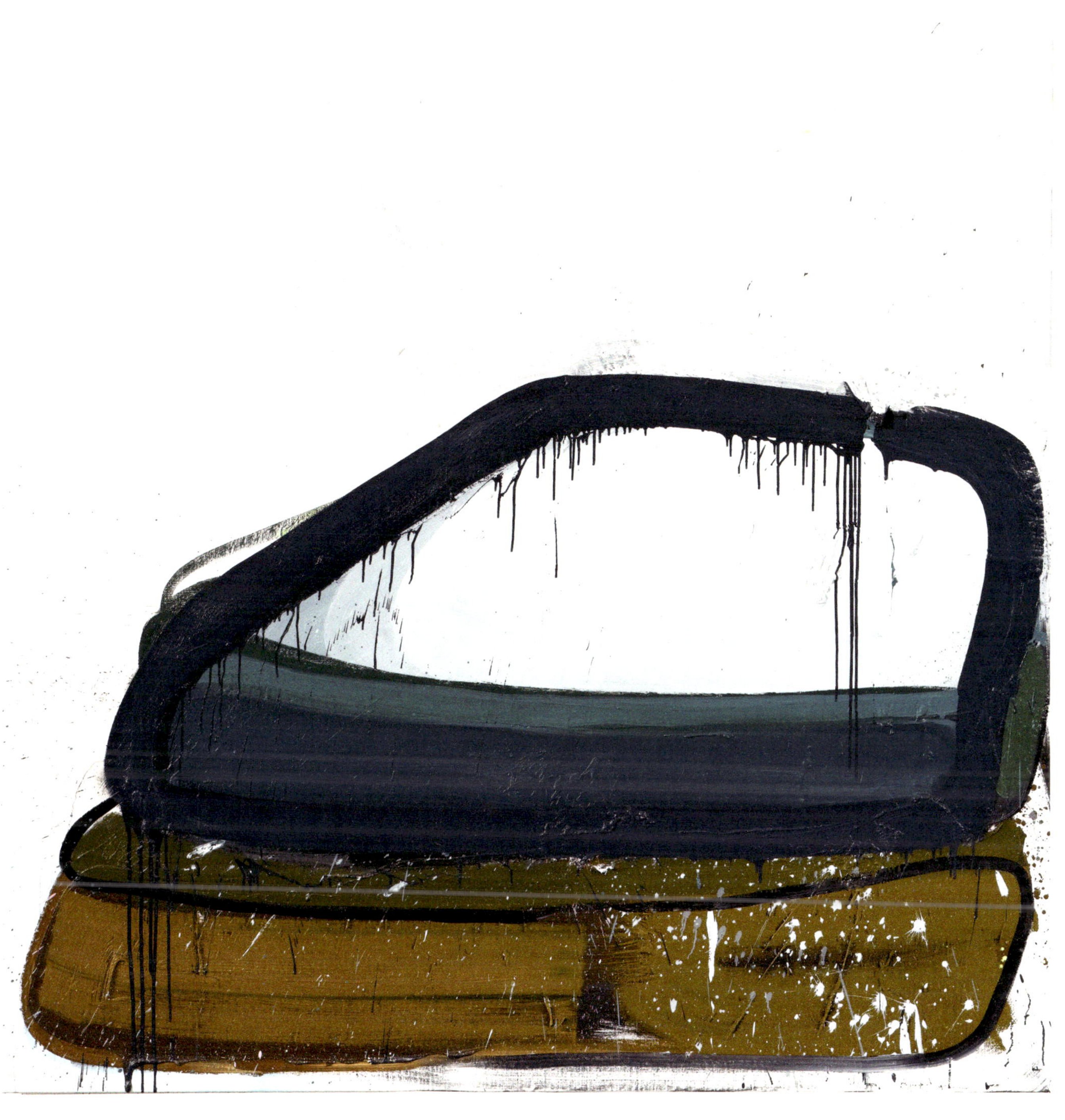

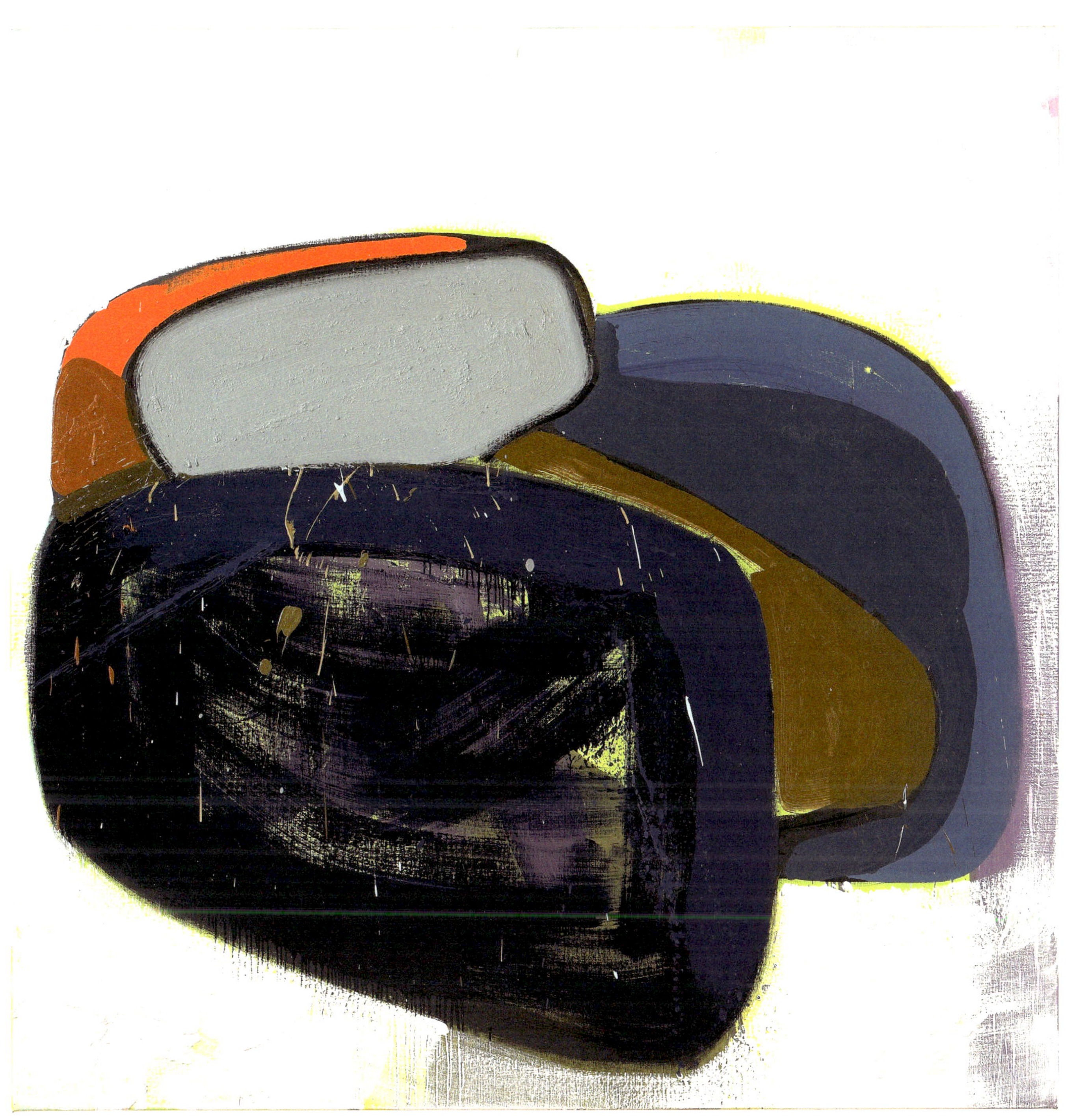

**Stol** 2006

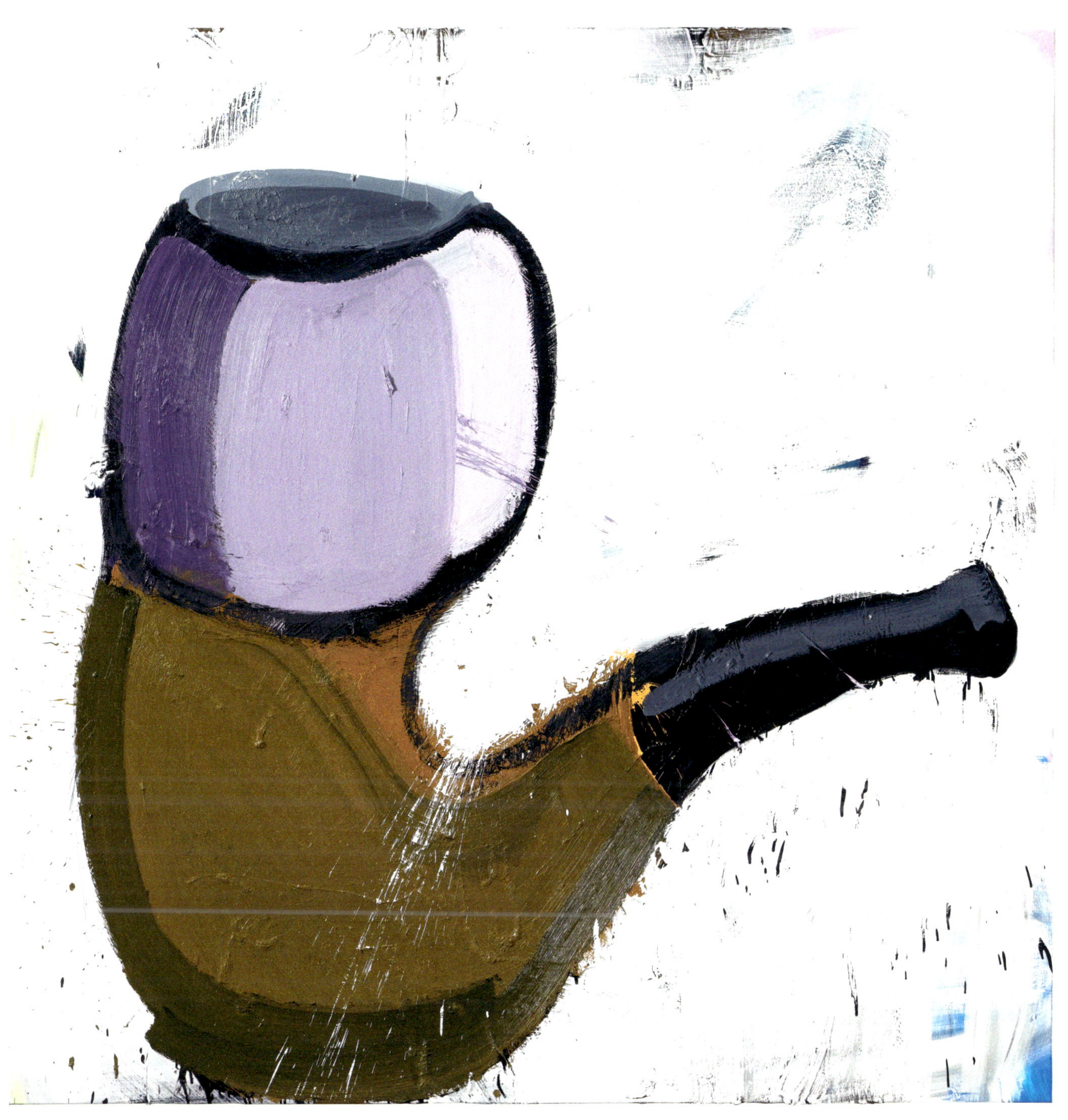

Pibe 2006

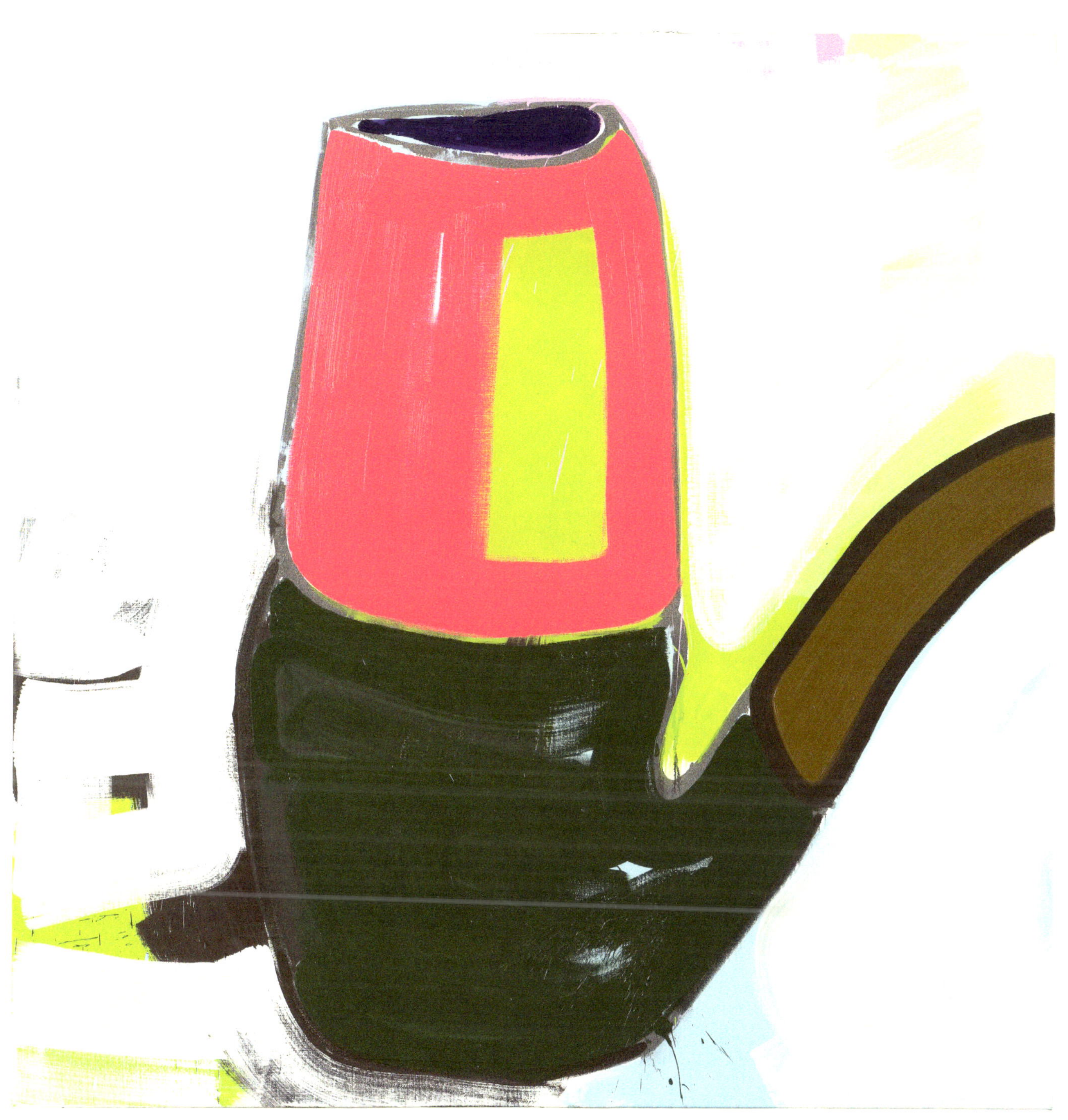

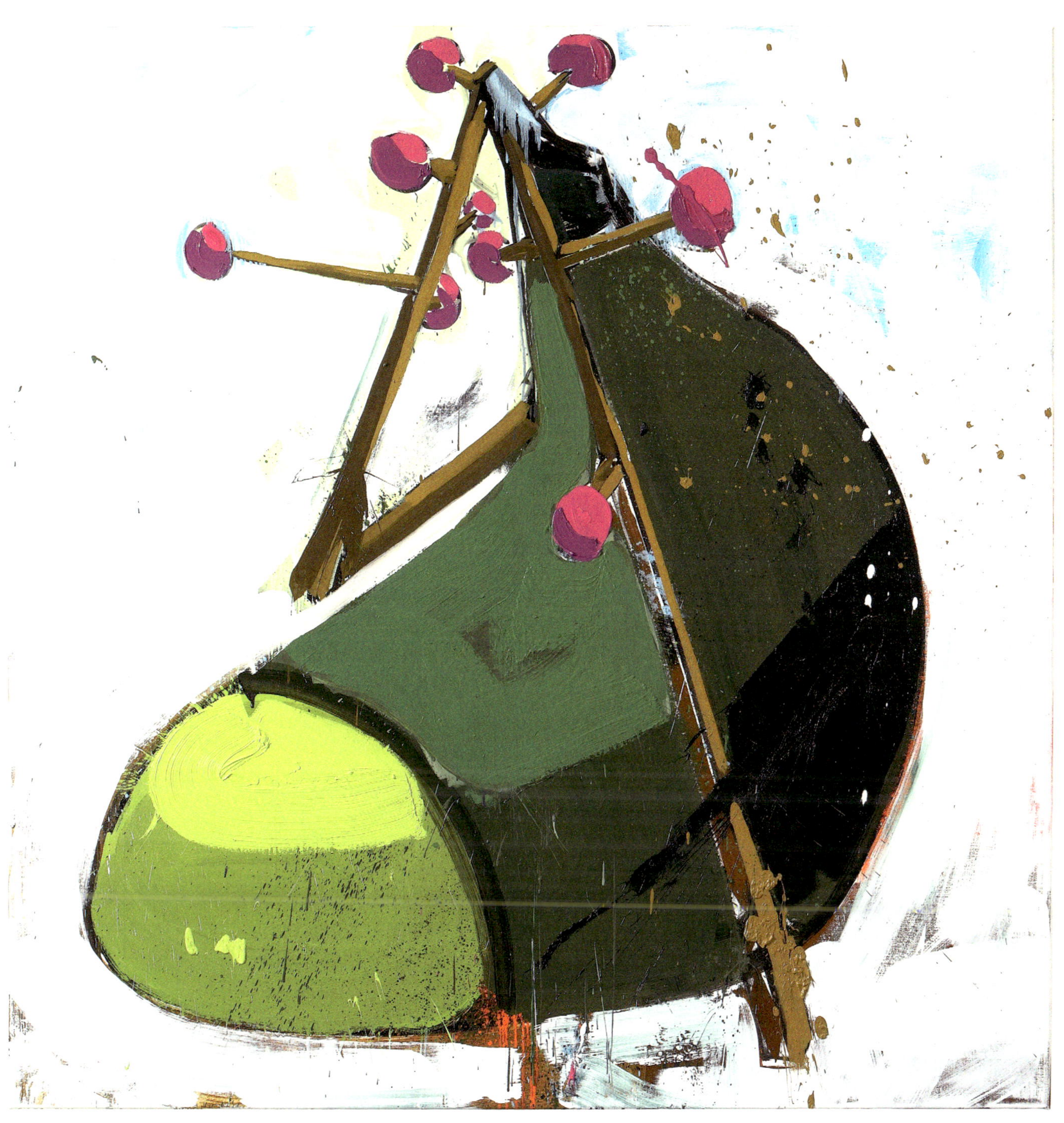

Vase 2006

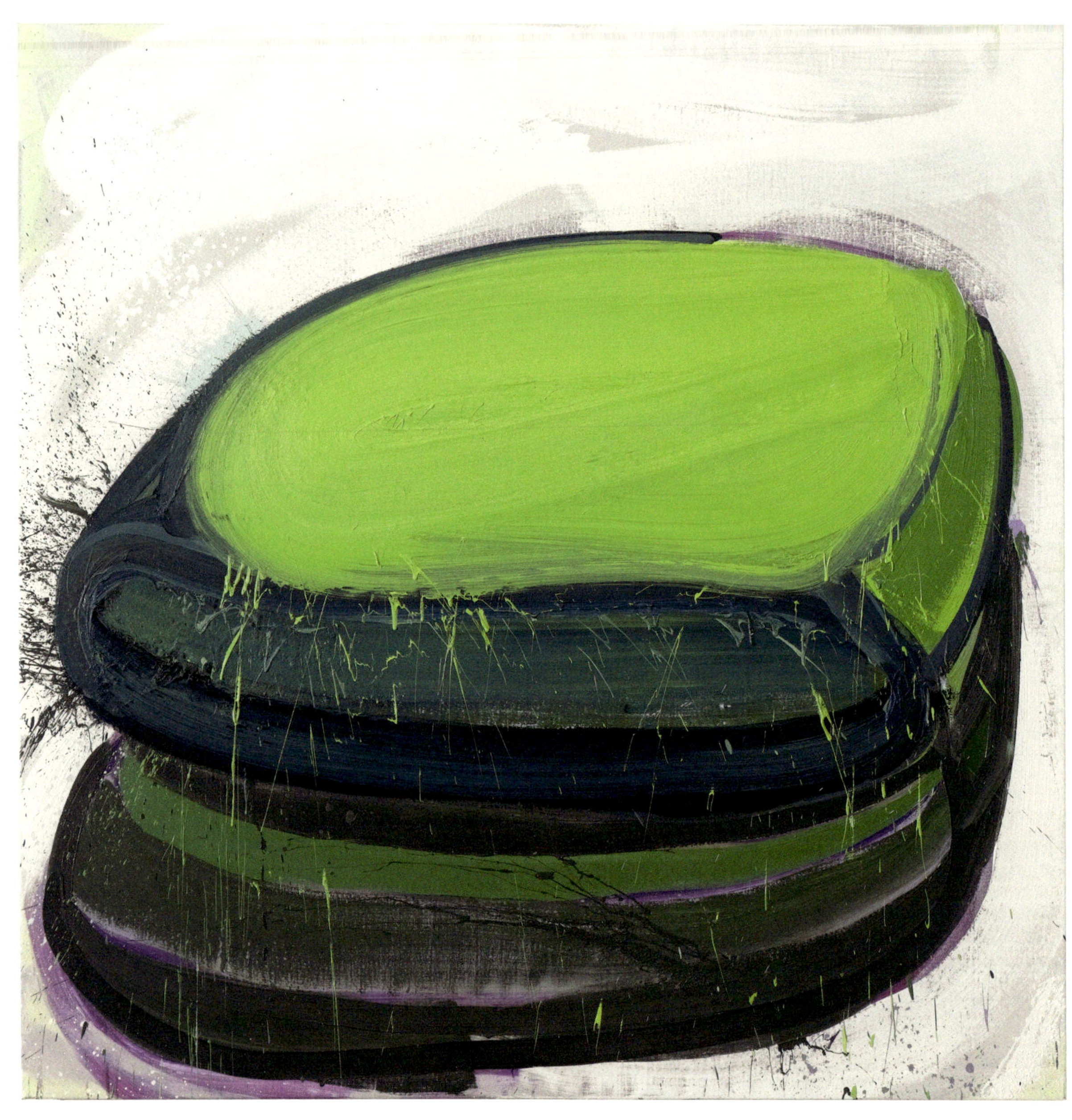



**Dobbeltmadras** 2008

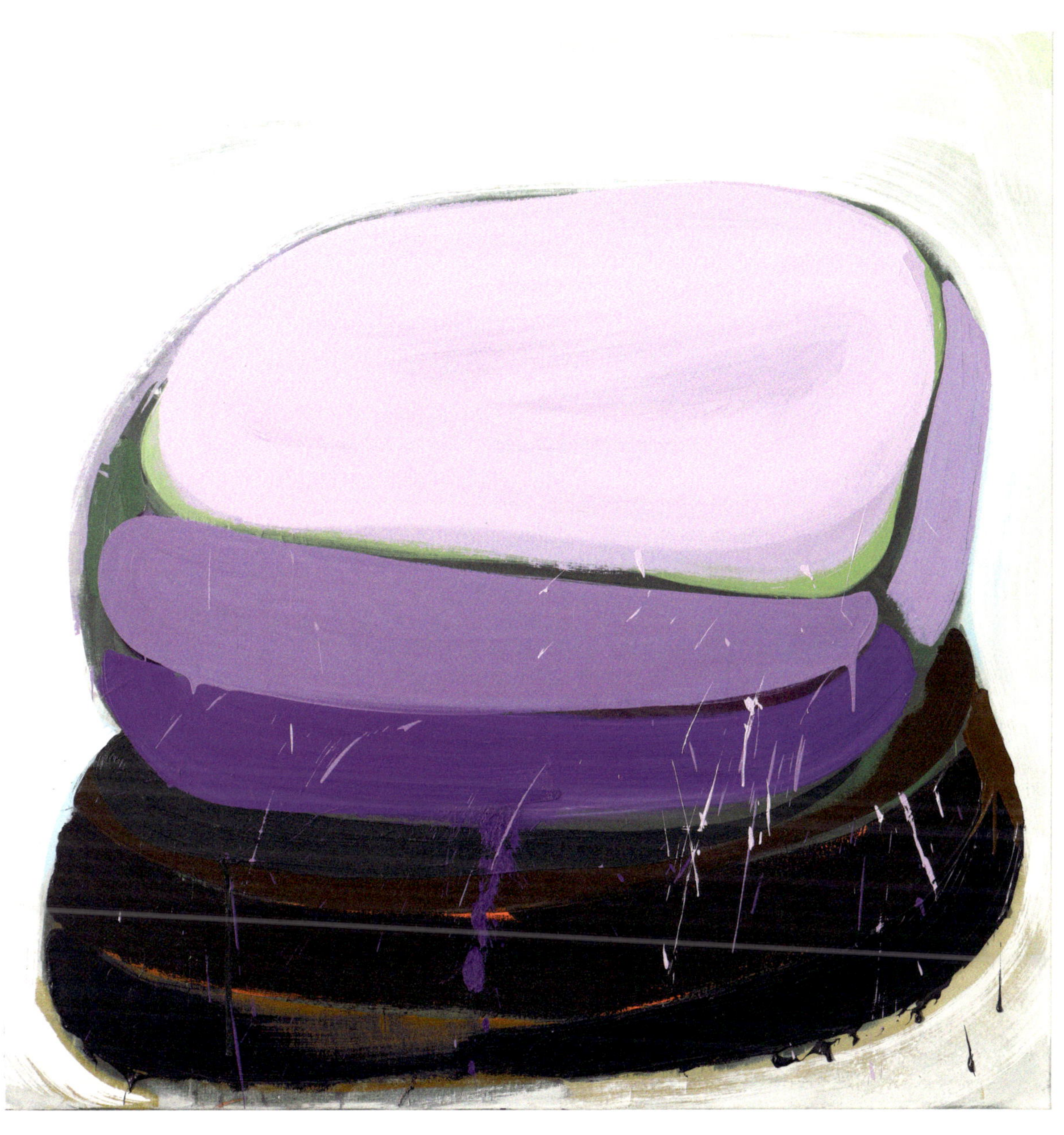

# Take Me Into

## Morten Buchs Werkserie von 2006

VON VIOLA WEIGEL

Die Malerei unterzieht sich zur Zeit einem „Bodycheck". Die Frage nach den künstlerischen Grundbedingungen eines Bildes wird von der heutigen Malergeneration mit selbstkritischem, teilweise auch ironischem Unterton gestellt. Morten Buch, geboren 1970 in Kopenhagen, zählt zu den skandinavischen Malern, die in den letzten Jahren mit Troels Wörsel (geb. 1950), Marcus Eek (geb. 1968) oder Tal R (geb. 1967) national und teilweise auch international zunehmende Aufmerksamkeit genießen. Es ist interessant zu beobachten, wie diese Künstler das Erbe des nordischen Expressionismus mit den Einflüssen der internationalen Avantgarde zu einer explizit „methodischen Malerei"[1] verschmelzen. Manche der Künstler sind aufgrund ihres expressiven Malstils mit den neo-expressionistischen deutschen „Wilden" der 80er-Jahre in Verbindung gebracht worden.[2] Doch hat deren existenzialistisches Pathos, wie wir auch in Buchs Werk beobachten werden, nichts mit den systematischen Ansätzen dieser Generation gemein, auch wenn der expressive Malgestus eines ihrer Hauptinstrumente bildet. In „Notes on Painting" räumt Troels Wörsel mit der Annahme auf, dass es so etwas wie „direkte Malerei"[3] gebe und stellt fest: „Painting is not *some direct method* of expressing emotions or states of mind. It only articulates *ideas* for these sorts of things. … Instead of finding pure expression for his emotions, he [der Künstler, vw] is constructing sign structures just like someone trying to paint a bowl of fruit."[4]

Eine Vase mit einem Blumengesteck stellt zunächst ein traditionelles und dazu noch gewöhnliches Genremotiv in der Kunst dar. Gleichzeitig markiert die Stilllebengattung den Auftakt der Moderne und Avantgarde um 1900. Denn Maler wie Edouard Manet, Paul Cézanne oder Pablo Picasso betrachteten das Alltagsmotiv als fruchtbares Experimentierfeld neuer Bildfindungen. Pablo Picasso schuf um 1907 keine Stillleben, sondern „he was making a picture"[5] und erfand mithilfe der traditionellen Gattung die Malerei und deren Wahrnehmung neu.[6] Buchs *Vase* (Abb. S. 21) konfrontiert uns schon allein durch ihre monumentalen Maße von 200 × 200 cm direkt und unvermittelt. Der weiße Hintergrund der Leinwand lässt ihre dunklen Umrisse wie einen Scherenschnitt überdeutlich hervortreten. Dass dies keine geläufige Repräsentation einer Vase darstellt, zeigt ihre eigentümliche bildnerische Sprache, die die vertraute Beziehung zwischen Behältnis (Vase) und Inhalt (Pflanze) umkehrt: Die braunen Stiele und gelben Blüten wirken künstlich und steif, idealistisch in der Form, und ragen wie kleine Rundplastiken aus dem Vasenhals. Organisch ist vielmehr der Vasenkörper selbst, der rechts knollenartig ausschwingt und im unteren Bereich, am Fuß, eine undefinierbare, monströse

# Your Skin

## Morten Buch's 2006 Series of Works

by Viola Weigel

Painting is currently undergoing a "bodycheck". The question surrounding the basic artistic conditions of a painting is one posed by today's generation of artists in self-critical and, at times, ironic undertones. Morten Buch, born in 1970 in Copenhagen, belongs to the group of Scandinavian painters who, including Troels Wörsel (b. 1950), Marcus Eek (b. 1968) and Tal R (b. 1967), have been attracting growing interest, both on a national level and, in some cases, also further afield. It is interesting to note the way in which these artists combine the legacy of Nordic Expressionism with the influences of the international avant-garde to form an explicitly "methodical" form of painting.[1] On the basis of their expressive style of painting, some of these artists have been associated with the German neo-expressionistic "Wilden" ("Wild Ones") of the 1980s.[2] And yet, as we will also be able to observe in Buch's work, their existential pathos has nothing in common with the systematic approaches of this generation; albeit the expressive artistic gesture constitutes one of their key devices. In "Notes on Painting" Troels Wörsel does away with the assumption that there is such a thing as "direct painting"[3] and states: "Painting is not *some direct method* of expressing emotions or states of mind. It only articulates *ideas* for these sorts of things. … Instead of finding pure expression for his emotions, he [the artist, vw] is constructing symbolic structures just like someone trying to paint a bowl of fruit."[4]

In the first instance a vase with a flower arrangement represents a traditional and moreover conventional artistic genre motif. At the same time, still life painting as a genre marks the lead-up to Modernism and the Avant-garde around 1900 with artists such as Edouard Manet, Paul Cézanne and Pablo Picasso perceiving the motif taken from everyday life as fertile ground for experimenting with new compositions. It was not still lifes that Pablo Picasso was painting around 1907; "he was making a picture"[5] and using the traditional genre, reinventing painting and the way it was perceived.[6] By virtue of its monumental size (200 × 200 cm) alone, we are brought squarely and abruptly face to face with Buch's *Vase* (ill. p. 21). Against the white background of the canvas, its dark outline is clearly defined as it were a cut-out. That this is no ordinary representation of a vase we are being presented with, is demonstrated by its peculiar artistic language that turns the familiar relationship between receptacle (vase) and content (plants) on its head: the brown stems and yellow blossom seem artificial and rigid, idealistic in form and rise out of the

blau-schwarze Form ausbildet. Die an sich regelmäßige Idealform einer Vase wird hier deutlich sichtbar in etwas Amorphes, in eine Anti-Vase, überführt. Trotz leichter Annäherungen ans moderne skandinavische Design, das organische Formen gerne mit Interieurgegenständen verbindet, wirkt dieser Teil konstruiert und gibt dem Ding eine unvorhersehbare formale Wendung sowie eine für seine Deutung folgenreiche Verschiebung. Wie soll man als Betrachter mit einer Vasendarstellung umgehen, in der kulturelle Konstruktion und zufällige Naturform einfach ihren Ort tauschen? Alle beschriebenen Elemente treiben die banale Darstellung einer Vase an die Grenzen ihrer Sichtbarkeit und ließen diese als übersteigerten Tagtraum erscheinen, wäre da nicht das sinnlich-konkrete Pulsieren der Farbmaterie auf der Leinwand. Das Traumgebilde wird „fleischgewordene" Malerei und karikiert dabei durchaus die distanzierte Aura ihres klassisch-perfekten Vorbildes.

### Die Rückkehr der Dinge

Die „Rückkehr der Dinge" auf dem Feld von Kunst und Wissenschaft ist nicht mit einer neoromantischen oder positivistischen Liebe zum Ding zu verwechseln, sondern wurde durch eine kritische Auseinandersetzung mit ihren eigenen Mitteln angeregt. 100 Jahre nach Picasso schreiben Künstler die Geschichte der Stilllebenmalerei auf unterschiedliche Weise fort. Für Maler wie Luc Tuymans stellte sich 2001 die grundsätzliche Frage, ob der Künstler nach dem 11. September Sujets aufgreifen darf, die mit dieser Form der Dingdarstellung und ihrer heilen Welt in Bezug stehen: Genauso wie Buch monumentalisierte Tuymans das Stilllebenmotiv, doch um mit diesem a-politischen Motiv die „Idee der Banalität" ins Extreme zu treiben (Abb. 1).[7] Die gegenwärtig zu beobachtende Beschäftigung mit dem Rohen, Handwerklichen und Basalen in der bildenden und angewandten Kunst scheint zu bestätigen,[8] dass die selbstgenügsamen „Simulacren" der Wirklichkeit (Jean Beaudrillard) keineswegs die Sehnsucht nach der Realität der Dinge und ihrer sinnlichen Materialität befriedigen konnten. Dinge sind interessant, weil sie ein komplexes Feld von kultureller Produktion ausbreiten. Durch „ihre Materialität wirken Dinge sinnlich einprägsam, durch ihre Form suggestiv, durch ihre Funktion alltagsnah und lebensweltlich plausibel".[9] Dagegen hebt Martin Heidegger in seiner Dingphilosophie „das Befremdende und Verschlossene im Wesen des Dinges" hervor.[10] Durch ihren gleichzeitigen Bezug zur realen wie symbolischen

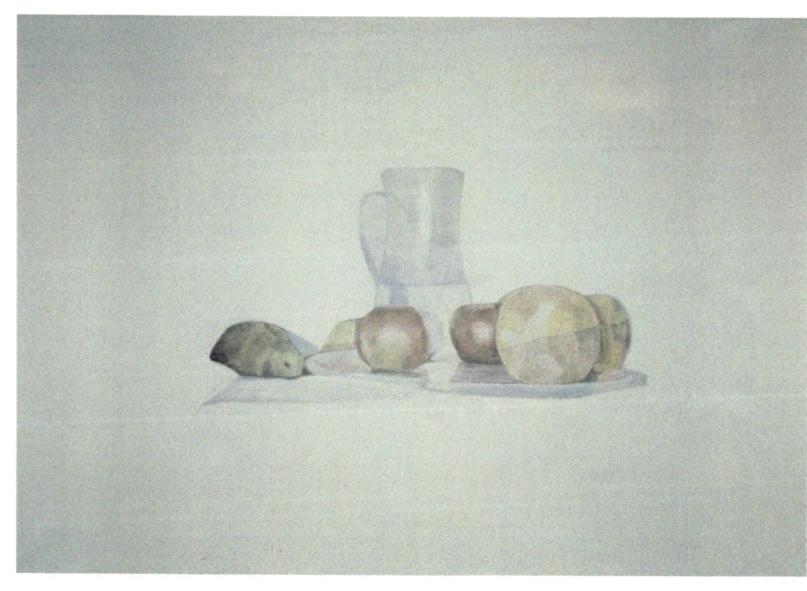

1 LUC TUYMANS, *Still-Life* | *Stillleben*, 2002, Öl auf Leinwand | Oil on canvas, 347 × 500 cm, Courtesy Zeno X Gallery Antwerp

neck of the vase like small sculptures in the round  It is rather the body of the vase itself that is organic in nature, swinging out bulbously to the right and in the lower area, at the base, developing into an indefinable, monstrous blue-black form. Here the recurring ideal shape of a vase per se is clearly turned into something amorphous, an anti-vase. Despite a faint resemblance to modern Scandinavian design, which likes to combine organic forms with interior objects, this part seems contrived and gives the thing a new and unanticipated twist in relation to form and also displaces it with significant consequence in terms of interpretation. As an observer, how is one supposed to deal with a representation of a vase, where cultural construction and random natural form simply swap places? All the elements described would push the banal representation of a vase to the limits of its visibleness and make these seem like an extreme daydream if it were not for the sensory reality of the pulsating colours on the canvas. The mirage becomes a painting made of "flesh and blood", thereby completely caricaturing the disassociated aura of its classically perfect prototype.

### The return of things

The "return of things" in art and science is not to be confused with a neo-romantic or positivistic liking for the thing, but was prompted rather by a critical confrontation with its own agency. 100 years after Picasso, artists continue the story of the still life in a variety of ways. 2001 posed artists like Luc Tuymans with the question of whether it was at all possible for an artist, in the aftermath of 9/11, to continue to address subjects that relate to this kind of representation of a thing with its intact world. Nonetheless, Tuymans, just like Buch, monumentalised the still life using its apolitical motif to push the "idea of banality" to the extreme (ill. 1).[7] The current preoccupation with raw materials, craftsmanship and the basics in the fine and applied arts[8] leads us to assume that the self-contained "simulacra" (Jean Beaudrillard) were in no way able to satisfy the yearning for the actuality of the things and their sensual materiality. Things are interesting, because of their complex ramifications for the scope of cultural production. By virtue of "their materiality, things make a sensory impression; by virtue of their form they are evocative; by virtue of their function suggestive of everyday life and plausible in terms of the world that we live in."[9] Martin Heidegger on the other hand, underlines in his philosophy of things the "alienating and withdrawn essence of the thing".[10] By simultaneously relating to both the real and the symbolic world, things present an extremely complicated and ambiguous system of signs. In contemporary art, however, and as we will come to see, it is precisely the *refusal* to render things symbolic that is characteristic.

The *Vase* belongs to a series of approximately 20 large-format oil paintings from 2006 portraying a deliberately narrow repertoire of motifs, such as vases, shoes, tents, mattresses and pipes. Compared to their familiar archetypes, the "brand" of objects selected

Welt stellen Dinge ein überaus kompliziertes und vieldeutiges Zeichensystem dar. In der zeitgenössischen Kunst wird allerdings gerade, wie wir noch beobachten werden, die *verweigerte* Zeichenhaftigkeit der Dinge charakteristisch.

Die *Vase* zählt zu einer Werkgruppe von circa 20 großformatigen Ölbildern von 2006, die ein bewusst schmales Repertoire von Motiven wie Vasen, Schuhe, Zelte, Matratzen oder Pfeifen zeigen. Gegenüber ihren vertrauten Vorbildern erscheinen die von Buch ausgewählten „Brands" von Objekten – kunsthistorisch und literarisch enorm aufgeladene Dinge – geradezu „schwanger" von Bedeutung bezüglich ihres Verhältnisses zur Bildgeschichte zu sein. Seit dem Surrealismus besitzt ein Schuh, etwa bei Meret Oppenheim, Fetischcharakter, die Darstellung einer Pfeife kann man nicht mehr betrachten, ohne an die kritische Sprachphilosophie von René Magritte zu denken und bei Francis Bacon dienen Matratzen als Plattformen für den eigentlichen Gewaltakt, nämlich den der Malerei.[11] Es ist zu fragen, ob sich Dinge deshalb – mehr als andere Bildmotive – dazu eignen, einen künstlerischen Keil zwischen Darstellung und Wirklichkeit zu treiben?

### Visualität als System

Mit Blick auf Morten Buchs vielseitiges Œuvre ist zu beobachten, dass die Spannung zwischen dem künstlerischen Prozess und der methodischen Versuchsanordnung der Bildmotive stets lebendig gehalten wird. Buch entwickelte sein künstlerisches Konzept kontinuierlich von Idee zu Idee, die der Künstler oft parallel umsetzt: „I think the reality in which we find ourselves … is something that I can best reflect in a multiplicity of techniques. I want to be able to make use of the computer and make things based on pixels, I would like to be able to make use of photographs … [as well as] to make rapidly drawn sketches and paint expressively."[12] Buchs erste professionelle Auseinandersetzung mit Kunst startet mit zwei bereits recht ausgereiften, installativen Werkgruppen Mitte der 90er-Jahre, *Éclairs* und *Zero Hour* (Abb. 2, 3). Ausgangspunkt ist die Farbmaterie, die Buch in Zusammenarbeit mit dem Künstler Jakob Leth Jensen nach einem Zufallsprinzip in dicken Schichten auf gleich große Spanholzplatten aufträgt und dadurch diverse Tiefendimensionen erzielt. Doch erst durch ihre jeweilige Anordnung an der Wand werden die frei kombinierbaren Platten zum räumlichen „Bildobjekt",

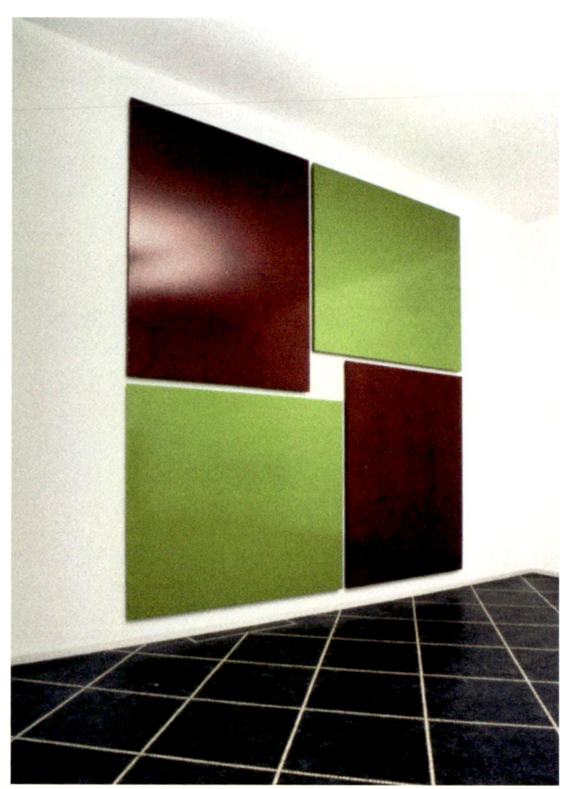

2    Morten Buch (mit | with Jakob Leth Jensen), *Éclair 4*, 1996/97, Öl auf MDF | Oil on MDF, 405 × 405 cm, Courtesy Galleri Susanne Ottesen, København

by Buch – things charged with both art-historical and literary significance – seem virtually 'pregnant' with meaning in terms of their relationship to the iconography. After Surrealism a shoe, a Meret Oppenheim one for instance, possesses a fetishistic quality; we can no longer look at the representation of a pipe without thinking of René Magritte's critical philosophy of language and Francis Bacon's mattresses serve as platforms for the real act of violence, namely painting.[11] This begs the question therefore, whether things – more so than other images in painting – lend themselves to driving a wedge between representation and reality?

## Visuality as system

The tension between the artistic process and the methodical experimental path by which he attempts to keep the motifs of his paintings alive – confirmed by a glance at Morton Buch's varied œuvre – was always an artistic stimulus. Buch's artistic concept has evolved consistently from one idea to the next and frequently executed by the artist at the same time: "I think the reality in which we find ourselves … is something that I can best reflect using a multiplicity of techniques. I want to be able to make use of the computer and make things based

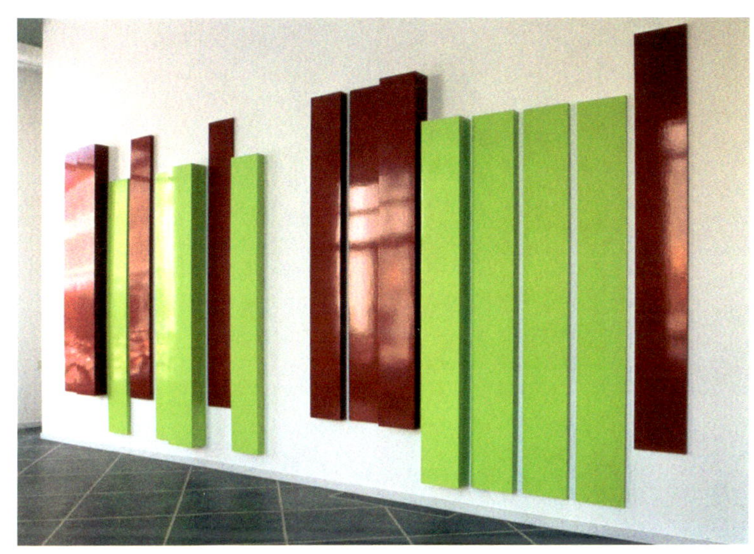

**3**    Morten Buch (mit | with Jakob Leth Jensen), *Zero Hour 1–2*, 1999, Öl auf MDF | Oil on MDF, 275 × 275 cm, Brask Collection & Courtesy Galleri Susanne Ottesen, København

on pixels, I would like to be able to make use of photographs … [as well as] to produce quick sketches and paint expressively."[12] Buch's first encounter with the art scene on a professional basis was with two already very mature installations in the 1990s, *Éclairs* and *Zero Hour* (ill. 2, 3). The starting point is the paint which Buch, in collaboration with the artist Jakob Leth Jensen, applies randomly and in thick layers onto equally-sized MDF boards, allowing him to achieve differing levels of three-dimensionality. However, it is only by being grouped in a particular arrangement on the wall that the panels – that can be assembled at will – become a 'pictorial object' in space and one that invites us to actively engage with it. As with the "Specific Objects" of American Minimal Art, differing sculptural qualities come to the fore according to the position from which we view the coloured panels. Their iridescently reflective surfaces mirror the surrounding space, causing the materiality of the colours to recede, and yet – when we step to the side – this materiality is tangibly

das zur aktiven Wahrnehmung auffordert. Wie die „Specific Objects" der amerikanischen Minimal Art treten je nach Position, von der aus wir die Farbtafeln betrachten, unterschiedliche räumliche Qualitäten hervor. Ihre schimmernd reflektierende Oberfläche spiegelt den Umraum wider und lässt die Materialität der Farbe zurücktreten, doch ist diese – wenn wir zur Seite treten – in der Tiefe der Reliefplatten real präsent. Die virtuose Variabilität der angeordneten Elemente in Farbe und Form wird durch die jeweilige Hängeordnung im Quadrat verabsolutiert. Bemerkenswert ist für die weitere künstlerische Entwicklung das Interesse von Buch, im Betrachter einen intensiven Widerstreit zwischen visuellen und – in der Leitung des Betrachters – körperbetont-haptischen Sinnen auszulösen.

Ab 2000 wendet sich Buch der Malerei auf Leinwand zu. Doch behält er die Spannung von Wiederholung und ästhetischer Differenz bei, die ein vielfältiges Sensorium der Betrachter ansprechen. Das Quadrat wird zum vorwiegenden Leitformat des Bildgevierts. Der mal ruhig handwerklich, mal spontan agierende Gestus zum Leitprinzip seiner Gestaltungsweise. Während die Pixelbilder von 2000 an ein nüchternes Bildraster bestimmt, dessen einzelne Quadrate in ihren Umrissen millimeterstark hervortreten (Abb. 4), werden die kleinformatigen Interieurs von 2001 aus tubendicken Linienfeldern „gebaut" (Abb. 5). Buch hebt 2003 sein Interesse an haptischen Oberflächen hervor: „I want to draw on references to both spaces and images surrounding us, to tactile surfaces, fashion, colours, design and so on."[13] Seine aktuellen Werkgruppen greifen einige der früheren Motive auf und wandeln sie ab, wie z. B. die zukunftsweisende Temperazeichnung *Schuh* von 2003. Die comicartige Skizze zeigt einen Fuß, der in einem seltsamen High-Heel-Schuh steckt. Dieser verliert an der Hacke gerade seine vertraute Form und läuft in einen amorphen Tropfen aus (Abb. 6). Der Schuh transformiert sich in sein dekonstruiertes, unbrauchbares Pendant und verschiebt unseren Blick von seiner Gebrauchsrolle zur autonomen Bildform oder, um mit Heidegger zu sprechen, vom einsatzbereiten „Zeug" zum selbstgenügsamen „Ding".[14] Man könnte auch formulieren: vom Haptischen zum Visuellen. Die nicht nur comic-, sondern auch künftig vermehrt blobartig auftretenden Motive weisen auf Buchs Wahrnehmung des Einflusses digitaler Techniken auf unsere Kultur hin, wie wir sie aus dem Einsatz digitaler CAD-Programme in der Architekturbranche oder von den Morphing-Techniken des Films (*Terminator II*, 1991) kennen. Die plötzliche,

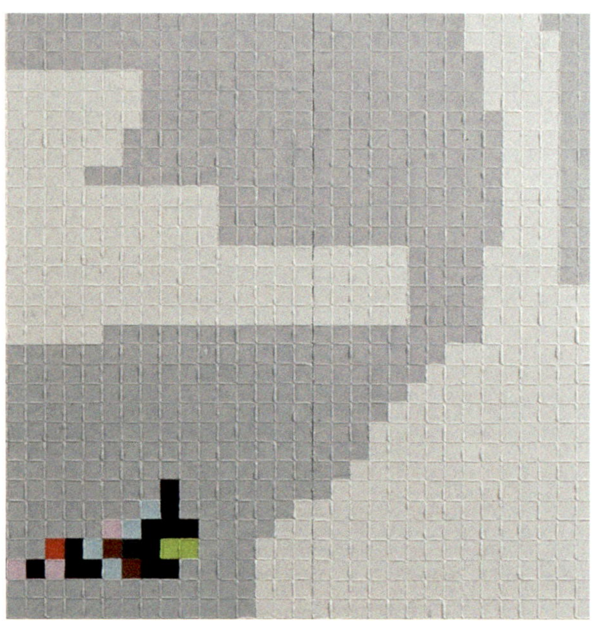

**4**  Morten Buch, *On the Floor*, (Detail), 2002, Öl auf Leinwand | Oil on canvas, 240 × 240 cm, Courtesy Galleri Susanne Ottesen, København

present in the depths of the relief panels. The brilliant variability of the positioned elements in terms of colour and form is rendered absolute by their particular arrangement in the square when they are hung. Noteworthy in relation to his continuing artistic development, is Buch's interest in triggering in the observer an intense conflict between the visual and – by directing the observer – the very physical haptic senses.

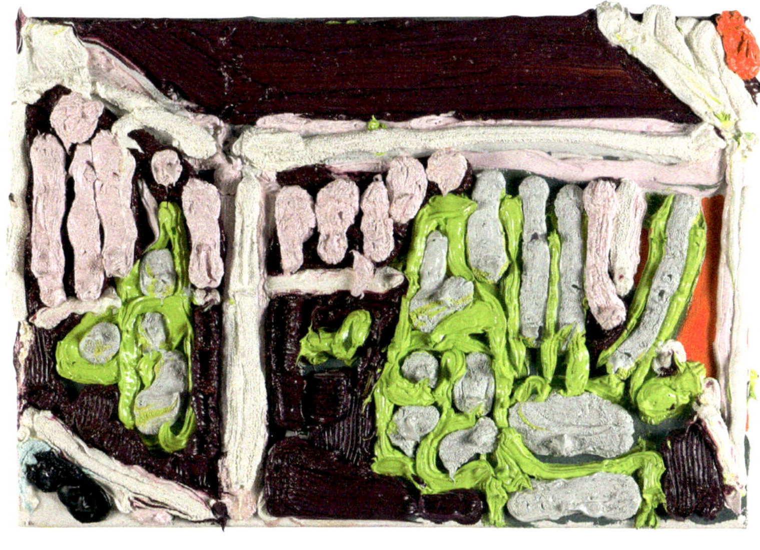

5    MORTEN BUCH, *Stilleben | Stillleben | Still Life*, 2001, Öl auf Leinwand | Oil on canvas, 24 × 36 cm, Private collection

From 2000 onwards, Buch turns to painting on canvas. Yet he retains the tension between reproduction and aesthetic difference that appeals to the observer's multi-tracked sensory apparatus. The square becomes the recurring format of the fourfold picture and the at times quietly skilful, at times spontaneously energetic manner, the central precept of his creative process. While the pixel images from 2000 give rise to a sober raster image, with the outline of each tiny individual square sharply defined (ill. 4), the small format interiors from 2001/02 are "constructed" from pipe-thick linear planes (ill. 5). In 2003, Buch reinforces his interest in haptic surfaces: "I want to draw on references to both spaces and images surrounding us, to tactile surfaces, fashion, colours, design and so on."[13] His recent works revisit some of the earlier motifs and modify them, as for instance in the trend-setting *Shoe*

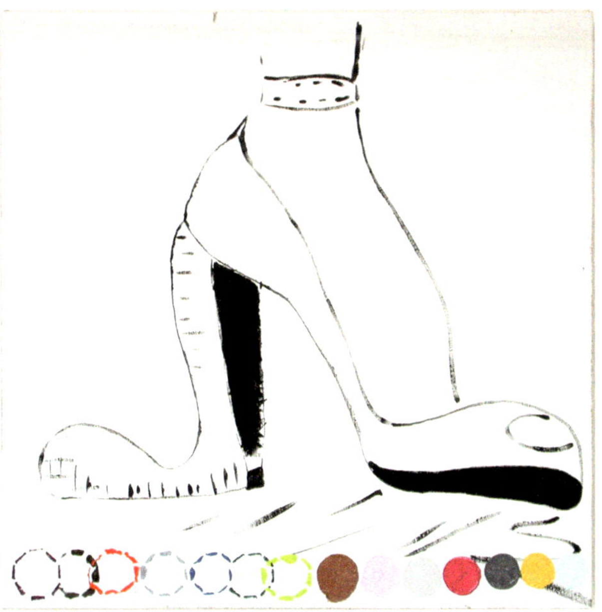

from 2003. This comic strip-like sketch shows a foot in a strange high-heel shoe. Right at the heel, this shoe loses it familiar form and tapers off into an amorphous blob (ill. 6). The shoe is transformed into its deconstructed, unusable counterpart and shifts our view away from its practical function to the autonomous form of the image or, in the words of Heidegger, from the operational "implement" to the self-contained "thing".[14] Alternatively, one could say: from the haptic to the visual. The appearance of not only comic, but in the future also increasingly blob-like motifs, are an indication of Buch's awareness of the influence of digital

6    MORTEN BUCH, *Sko | Schuh | Shoe*, 2003, Tempera und Öl auf Leinwand | Tempera and oil on canvas, 40 × 40 cm, Courtesy Galleri Susanne Ottesen, København

gleichsam surrealistische Verwandlung an einem Motiv zu zeigen, wird ein Bildprogramm, das
für die seit 2006 entstehende Werkgruppe leitend ist. Figuren oder Personen fehlen hier ganz,
doch taucht Körperlichkeit in anderer Form in der Malerei wieder auf. Denn, so stellte schon
Bruno Latour fest: „Dinge existieren nicht, ohne voller Menschen zu sein."[15] Buchs Thema von
1997 bis 1999 „das Bild als Objekt" (the very object of the picture)[16] zu behandeln, verlagert sich
nun auf die komplexe Anschauung zwischen Farbspur und Formausdehnung, die den Blick
durch den Farbauftrag und die subjektive Pinselführung auf das leiblich-sinnliche Potenzial der
Leinwand lenkt. „Der Maler bringt seinen Körper ein, sagt Valéry. Und in der Tat kann man sich
nicht vorstellen, wie ein reiner Geist malen könnte. Indem der Maler der Welt seinen Körper
leiht, verwandelt er die Welt in Malerei."[17]

### Die Präsenz der Dinge

Auf der weißen, wie ausgeräumt erscheinenden Bildfläche entwickeln Buchs präzise umrissene
Motive einen monumentalen und allgemeingültigen Bildstatus. In der klassischen Moderne
erhielt die Dingdarstellung erstmals mit van Gogh eine eigenständige Bedeutung und befrei-
te sich endgültig von jeder über sie hinausweisenden symbolischen Lesart.[18] Doch erst die
quadratische Leinwand verleiht den Motiven ihren hervorstechenden ikonenhaften Charakter. Durch das ausgeglichene Format, das beispielsweise auch Andy Warhol für seine Portraits
einsetzte, können die Arbeiten die Spannung zwischen universaler Form und Vieldeutigkeit
ausspielen. Die Quadratform stellt seit Malewitschs Ölbild *Schwarzes Quadrat* von 1915 eine
Nullform von Malerei und damit quasi die Embryonalform aller konzeptuellen Bildideen dar.[19]
Das statische Quadrat eignet sich als idealer Ort ungelenkten und meditativen Schauens, das
sich zwischen Bildzentrum und Rand bewegt. Doch lässt die lebendige Farbtextur der Werke
diese visuelle Offenheit überhaupt zu?

### Auf den Leib gerückt: „Take me into your skin"[20]

Der Phänomenologe Maurice Merleau-Ponty beschreibt eingehend, wie die Wahrnehmung
der sichtbaren Seite eines Dinges sich notwendigerweise mit dessen unsichtbarer Rückseite
verbindet. „Es reicht, dass ich von einer Seite die Rückseite des Handschuhes sehe, die sich auf
die Vorderseite legt, dass ich eine *durch* die andere berühre …: das ist Chiasmus." Die Dinge
verdoppeln sich jeweils in ihr Innen und ihr Außen.[21] Das Motiv der Matratze verkörpert wohl
am anschaulichsten die Verschränkung von psychischem Innen- und physischem Außenraum
im Bildgefüge. Deshalb stellt es ein recht junges Motiv in der Kunstgeschichte dar und taucht
als eigenständiger Bildgegenstand erst mit der Begründung der Psychoanalyse und der Ent-
deckung des Unbewussten durch Sigmund Freud um 1900 auf. Im Zuge der fortschreitenden
Entblößung und Nacktheit des Menschen verändert sich auch dessen Verhältnis zum Raum,
was sich grundlegend auf die innerbildnerische Beziehung von Figur und Grund auswirkt.
Bei Edvard Munch kündigt sich die Verschränkung von Physis und Psyche wohl zuerst an: In

technology on our culture, as is familiar to us from the use of CAD programmes in architecture or the morphing techniques used in films (*Terminator II, 1991*). The impact of a sudden, as it were surrealist, alteration of a motif becomes a pictorial agenda that has been central to his works from 2006 onwards. People or figures are entirely absent in the painting; however physicality emerges in another form. Bruno Latour put it this way: "Things do not exist unless they are human beings."[15] Buch's subject matter between 1997 and 1999, "the very object of the picture",[16] now focuses on the complex perspective amid the trace of colour and the development of form that, through the application of colour and the subjective brushwork, directs the eye towards the physical-sensual potential of the canvas. "The painter invests his own body, says Valery. Indeed, it is difficult to imagine how the intellect alone could paint. By lending his body to the world, the artist transforms the world into paintings."[17]

### The presence of things

On the white canvas, with its appearance of having been stripped bare, Buch's precisely defined motifs evolve a monumental and universally valid representational status. In classical modernism, the representation of a thing first becomes significant in its own right with the work of van Gogh, finally extricating itself from all symbolic readings.[18] However, it was the square canvas that first lent the motifs their impressive iconic character. As a result of the well-balanced format that was also, for instance, made use of by Andy Warhol in his portraits, the artworks are able to play out the tension between universal form and ambiguity. Ever since Malewitsch's oil painting *Black Square* from 1915, the square format has constituted a zero point in art and thereby the embryonic form as it were of all conceptual representational ideas.[19] The rigid square provides the ideal place for autonomous and meditative viewing, moving between the centre and the edge of the painting. Does the vivid colour texture of a work, however, permit this visual openness at all?

### Put under pressure: "Take me into your skin"[20]

The phenomenologist Maurice Merleau-Ponty describes in detail how the perception of the visible side of a thing is necessarily linked to its invisible reverse side: "It is sufficient that from one angle I see the back of the glove that is lying on its front, that I touch one side *through* the other …: that is chiasmus." Things become duplicated, inside and outside.[21] The mattress motif possibly embodies most vividly the crossover of the psychological interior and physical exterior within the framework of the painting. It is therefore a rather young motif in art history and only emerges as a symbolic image in its own right with the establishment of psychoanalysis and the discovery of the unconscious by Sigmund Freud around 1900. In the course of the explorations of such revelations and nakedness of mankind, the latter's relationship to space also changes, fundamentally

seinen Interieurs stellt das Bett als
eingegrenzte Zone nicht einfach
ein in den Raum gestelltes Möbel
dar, sondern verkörpert auch den
eingeschränkten, psychischen Innenraum der Person, die dort sitzt.
In Max Liebermanns *Samson und
Delila* von 1901 (Abb. 7) gerät die Matratze zur Plattform des Kampfs der
Geschlechter um 1900. Schon hier
drängt der neutrale graue Hintergrund die Figuren nach vorne, zum
Betrachter hin, und bezieht diesen
aktiv ins Geschehen mit ein. Als Ort
der (malerischen) Unfälle wird das
Bett bei Francis Bacon ebenfalls zur

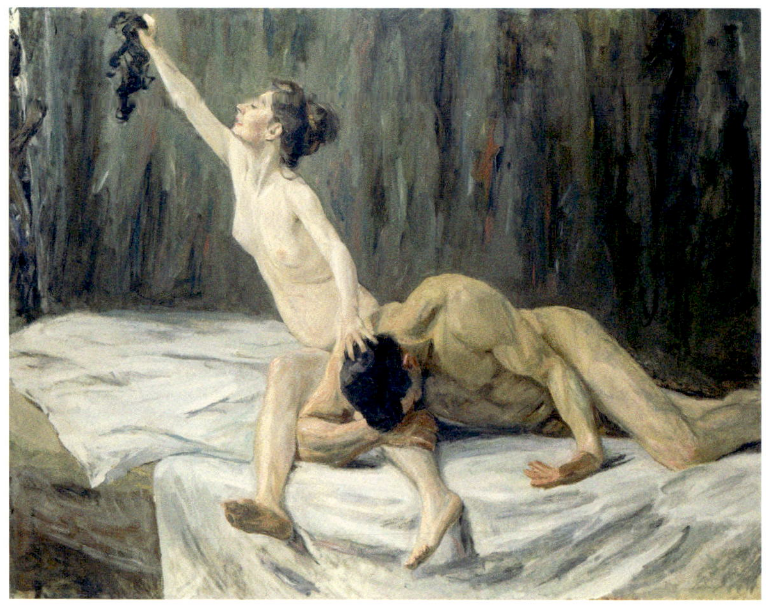

**7**  Max Liebermann, *Samson und | and Delila*, 1901, Öl auf Leinwand | Oil on canvas, 151,2 x 212 cm, Städel Museum, Frankfurt/M.

Plattform für die Einheit von Leben und Malakt, wo sich die „earthly pleasures" (weltlichen Freuden) in potenziell unkontrollierbare Ereignisse umkehren.

Buchs Serie von Matratzen von 2006 bis 2008 bilden einen Gegenpart zu seinen tendenziell tektonischen Schuhmotiven, die sich nach allen vier Seiten ausbreiten und mehr Bewegungs-spielraum besitzen. Durch ihre behäbige Präsenz versperrt die *Doppelmatratze,* 2006 (Abb. 8 und S. 27), uns den Weg und rückt uns „auf den Leib".[22] Eingezwängt in einen engen Bildraum liegt die Form direkt im Blickfeld. An diesem Ding kommen wir weder „vorbei" noch „hindurch". Sie fordert uns auf, ein Verhältnis – gutes oder schlechtes – zu ihr zu entwickeln. Widerstand ist zwecklos, denn ihre gedrängte Räumlichkeit im Bildgeviert und ihre erdig-rohe Farbigkeit ver-führen uns sofort. Der helle Hintergrund, der das Motiv umgibt, ist keineswegs eine klinisch-weiße Fläche, sondern besteht aus einem Schleier übereinandergelagerter Farbschichten, die von hellen zu immer dunkleren Farben wechseln, je näher sie der Bildoberfläche kommen. Wie der Golem scheint sich das jeweilige Motiv aus allen Farben der Oberflächen, die sich während des Malprozesses übereinanderschichten, herauszuschälen und zur Erscheinung zu bringen. Da und dort blitzt ein Komplementärkontrast – Rot/Grün oder Gelb/Violett – auf, wenn zwei Farbverläufe zusammentreffen, und überstrahlt wie in der *Vase* oder im *Zelt* das umliegende Farbfeld (Abb. S. 24/25). Rot, das sich unmittelbar mit dem Inkarnat der Haut oder Fleisch ver-bindet, wird in der *Matratze* hinter die neutraleren Töne wie Braun, Grau und Blau gelegt, sodass es umso intensiver hervorbricht. Entscheidend ist nun die durch das Rot sichtbar ge-machte Falte, die zwischen den Matratzen der Doppelmatratze liegt. An diesem „Knotenpunkt", am Umbruch von der Innen- zur Außenseite des Dings, manifestieren sich die „möglichen" Räume in diesem Bild und die Verbindung von Sichtbarem und Unsichtbarem. „Diese Falte", so

affecting the relationship between figure and background within the painting. The first manifestation of the crossover of physical nature and psyche is perhaps that seen in the work of Edvard Munch: in his interiors, the bed as a finite zone does not simply constitute a piece of furniture placed in the room; it also embodies the constrained inner space of the person sitting there. In Max Liebermann's *Samson and Delilah* from 1901 (ill. 7), the mattress becomes a platform for the battle of the sexes around 1900. Here the neutral gray background is already edging the figures into the foreground, towards the observer and actively drawing him/her into events. As the site of (artistic) failures, in the works of Francis Bacon, the bed also becomes a platform for the unity of life and the act of painting where the "earthly pleasures" turn into potentially uncontrollable events.

Buch's series of double-mattresses between 2006 and 2008 create a counterpart to his tectonically predisposed shoe motifs that extend out in all four directions, boasting greater scope for movement. By means of its imposing presence, the *Double-mattress*, 2006 (ill. 8 and p. 27), obstructs us and "puts us under pressure".[22] Forced into a narrow pictorial space, the form lies directly in our field of vision. We can neither "get past" this thing nor can we go "through" it. It exhorts us to form a relationship with it – good or bad. Resistance is futile as its crushed spatiality in the fourfold of the painting and its earthen-red colour seduces us at once. The light background surrounding the motif is by no means a clinically white surface, but rather it consists of a veil of layers of colour superimposed upon one another, changing from light to increasingly darker colours the closer to the surface of the painting they reach. Like the golem, the respective motif seems to emerge in its manifest form out of all of the surface colours that become layered on top of one another in the course of the painting process. Here and there a complementary contrast appears out of the blue – red/green or yellow/violet – when two colour gradients meet and eclipse the surrounding colour field, as in the *Vase* (ill. p. 21) or in the *Tent* (ill. p. 24/25). In the *Mattress* the colour red, directly associated with the tones of skin or flesh is laid down behind the more neutral tones, such as brown, green and blue in order that it strikes you all the more intensely. Of crucial significance is the crease exposed by the red colour that lies between the mattresses that make up the double mattress. At this "junction", at the break between the interior and exterior aspects of the thing, the "potential" spaces in this painting become manifest, the visible

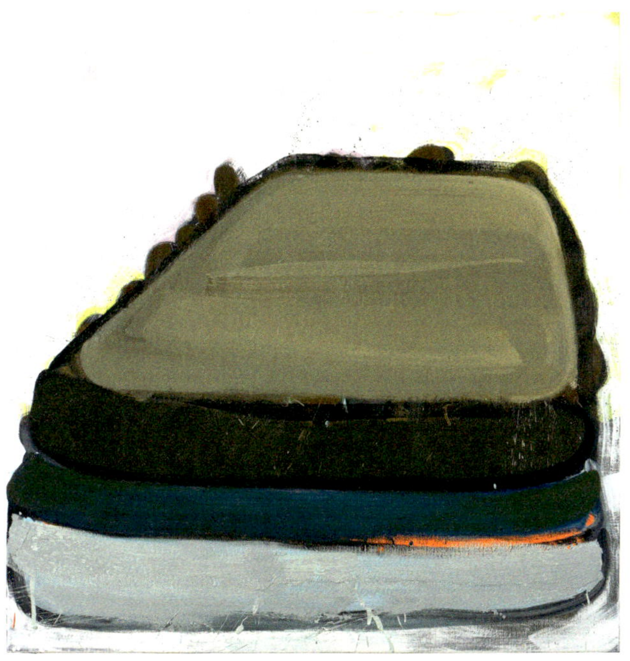

8   Morten Buch, *Dobbeltmadras | Doppelmatratze | Double-mattress*, 2006, Öl auf Leinwand | Oil on canvas, 200 × 200 cm, Danish Arts Council

Merleau-Ponty, „diese zentrale Höhlung im Sichtbaren, die mein Sehen ausmacht, diese beiden spiegelbildlichen Reihen von Sehendem und Sichtbarem, von Berührendem und Berührtem bilden ein wohlverbundenes System".[23]

Wie die Motivwahl ist die Werkgruppe durch eine schmale Farbpalette charakterisiert und durch kühle und warme Pastelltöne geprägt.[24] Farbe schmückt nicht nur die Oberfläche des Dargestellten, sondern ist ein Element, das den Körper in seiner mehrdimensionalen Körperlichkeit erscheinen lässt. Sie fügt sich zu Oberflächen zusammen, unterscheidet sich quasi als „Haut" von einem Inneren, Grund oder Dahinter – dem Fleisch der Leinwand. Doch um diese Körper kann man nicht herumgehen, sondern nur ahnen, wo sie – von Blicken verschlossen – Innenräume ausbilden. Der Umraum fordert vor allen Dingen in den letzten Werken wie dem steilen, rosafarbenen *Schuh* von 2008 (Abb. S. 40/41) Beachtung, wo die sonst wohlig-wattige Zone die klaustrophobische Note eines Horror Vacui gewinnt, so dass diese eher zum Widerpart des Dargestellten wird. Angesichts der *Matratze,* 2006, wird der Zusammenhang von Motiv und malerischer Form unmittelbar einsichtig. Denn das Blättrige und Geschichtete der gemalten Oberfläche geht mit dem Inhalt des Dargestellten („Doppelmatratze") einher. Schichtungen von Formen sind mit den Schichtungen von breiten Pinselstrichen identisch. Ein einzelner breiter Pinselstrich materialisiert eine Matratze. Betrachtet man die anderen Werke, so fällt das Prinzip der dreifachen Schichtung in tonaler Farbabstufung auch bezogen auf die Flächen- und Volumengestaltung einer Form auf: Ein dunkles, mittleres und helles Violett formen die kissenartige Brosche auf dem *Schuh,* 2006 (Abb. S. 15); ein dunkles, mittleres und helles Grün ein Element im *Sofa,* 2007 (Abb. S. 88/89), oder die *Matratze,* 2008 (Abb. S. 38), selbst. Die Problematik der Oberfläche, so der Kunsthistoriker Georges Didi-Huberman, haben die Maler des 19. Jahrhunderts durch die „Blättrigkeit, Schicht, Dichte" zurückgelassen und erstmals so etwas wie „Raumintervalle" (Jean Clay) geschaffen, „wodurch die Tiefen ‚emporsteigen, durchbrechen, eine Oberfläche bilden'".[25] Die bezüglich der ersten Werkgruppe *Zero Hour* erwähnte „fleischliche" Komponente der Malstruktur taucht hier in veränderter Gestaltungsweise wieder auf. Risse, Störungen und Brüche in der glatten Farbfläche werden notwendiger Teil des Malaktes. Doch welches Formkalkül leitet Buchs Malerei? – Wohl nicht der existenzialistische oder pathetische Umgang mit den Farbschründen wie im Informel. Doch auch die farbgesättigte Farbfeldmalerei (Mark Rothko) oder die kühlen Formen der Shaped Canvases (Frank Stella, Ellsworth Kelly) oder von Blinky Palermo können nur als loser, nicht wirklich befriedigender Vergleich dienen.

### Kalkulierte Plötzlichkeit: Der Klecks

In der traditionellen Stilllebenmalerei kreist oft ein Schmetterling über dem auf dem Tisch arrangierten Gemüse, oder eine Fliege sitzt auf den Früchten. Die Insekten weisen nicht nur auf die Vergänglichkeit (vanitas) der dargestellten Genüsse hin, sondern veranschaulichen auch die Echtheit und damit Raffinesse ihres Gemaltseins (Abb. 9, S. 58). An die Stelle der beweglichen Fliege rückt in der Gegenwartskunst die fließende und tropfende Farbmaterie. Der ge-

and the invisible. "This fold", Merleau-Ponty wrote, "this central void in the visible that constitutes my seeing, both of these mirror-like sequences of the seeing and the visible, of the touching and the touched form a well-integrated system".[23]

As with the choice of motifs, the works have a recognisably narrow palette and are characterised by cool and warm pastel shades.[24] Colour does not merely embellish the surface of the represented object; it is a factor that the physical form in its multidimensional physicality causes to become visible. Colour coalesces and constructs surfaces, is distinguishable, as a quasi "skin", from the interior, background, or a beyond – the flesh of the canvas. However, we cannot circumvent these physical forms, we can only begin to know where they – hidden from view – form interior spaces. The surrounding space, above all in the most recent works, such as the stunning pink *Shoe* from 2008 (ill. p. 40/41), demands our attention, with the remaining comfortingly woolly zone acquiring the claustrophobic note of a horror vacui and making it more like an adversary to the portrayed object. When faced with the *Mattress,* 2006, the correlation of motif and artistic form becomes immediately comprehensible since the flaky and layered nature of the painted surface goes hand in hand with the subject matter portrayed ("Double Mattress"). The layered construction of forms is identical with the layered construction of the broad brush strokes. One single broad brush stroke materialises a mattress. If we consider the other works then the principle of the triple layering in tonal gradation of colour in relation also to the formation of surfaces and volumes of a form is also striking: a dark, middle and light violet form the cushion-like clasp on the *Shoe,* 2006 (ill. p. 15); a dark, middle and light green, an element of *Sofa,* 2007 (ill. p. 88/89), and then there is the *Mattress,* 2008 (ill. p. 38) itself. According to the art historian Georges Didi-Huberman, by virtue of the "flakiness, the layer, the density", the painters of the 19th century have left the problematic nature of surfaces behind and have for the first time created something along the lines of "spatial intervals" (Jean Clay), through which the depths "climb, break through, form a surface".[25] The "flesh and blood" component of the painting structure mentioned in relation to the first group of works *Zero Hour* turns up here again with a variation on the creative approach. Cracks, disruptions and fractures in the smooth colour surface necessarily become part of the act of painting. What deliberation of form is it though that governs Buch's painting? Certainly not the existential or emotional engagement with the fissures in the colour as in informal art. And yet, even the colour-saturated Colour Field painting (Mark Rothko) or the cold forms of the Shaped Canvases (Frank Stella, Ellsworth Kelly) and Blinky Palermo can only serve as loose and not exactly very satisfactory comparisons.

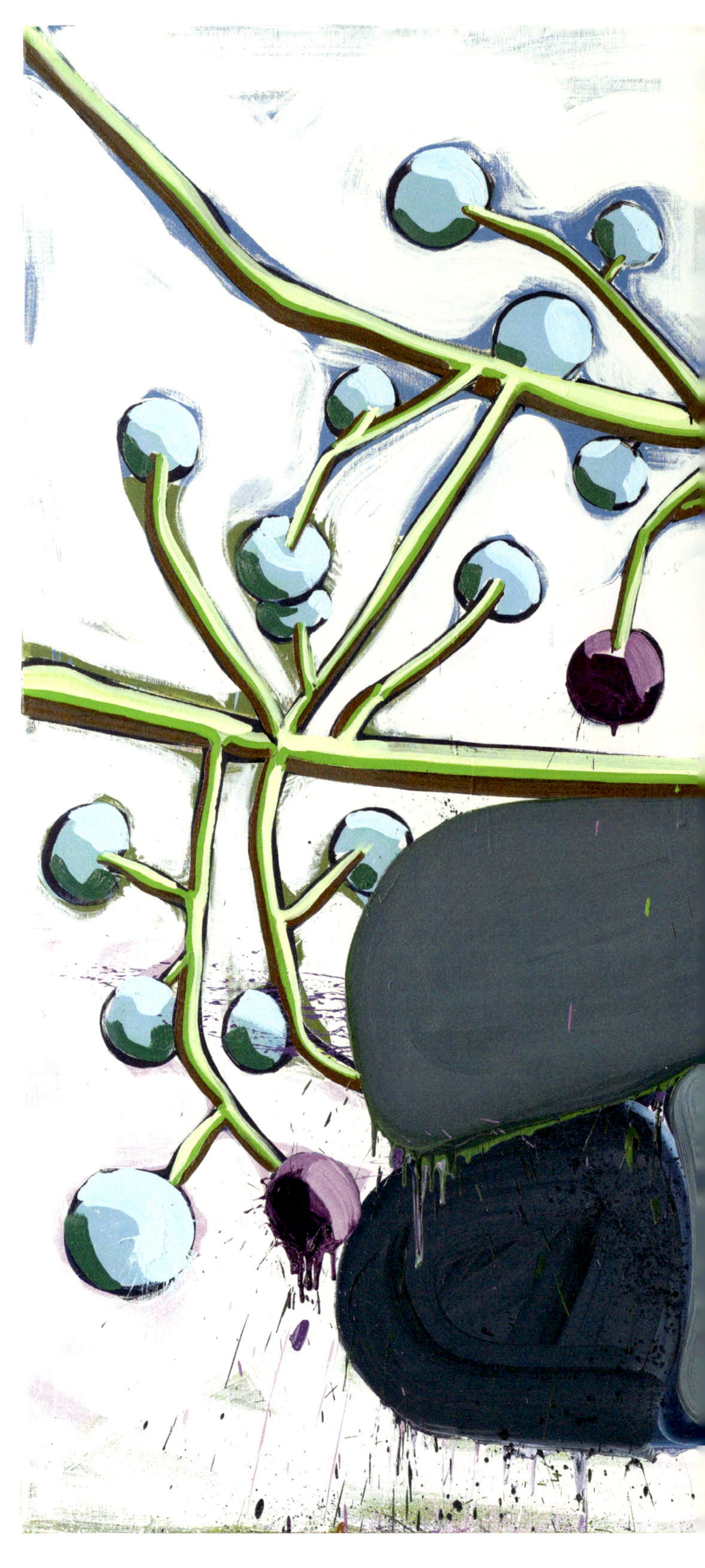

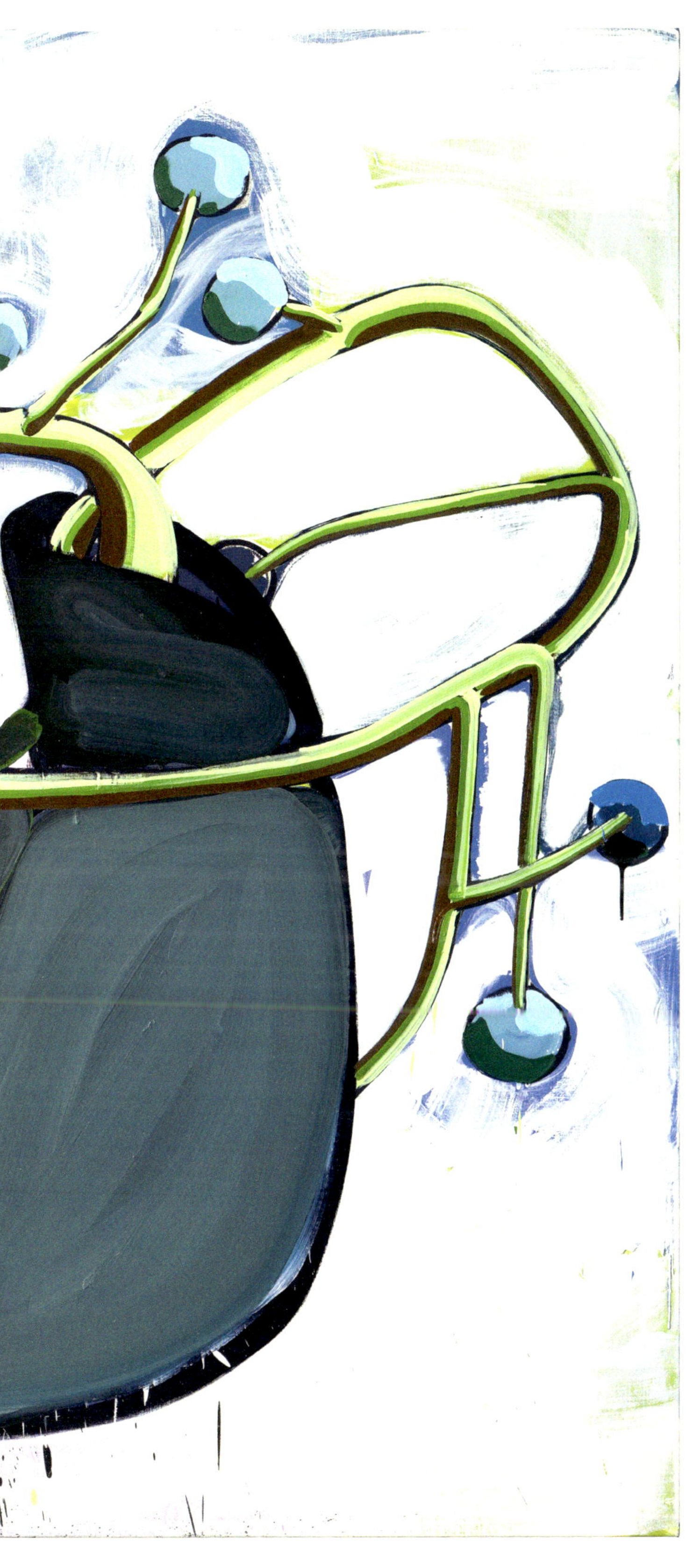

Vase 2006

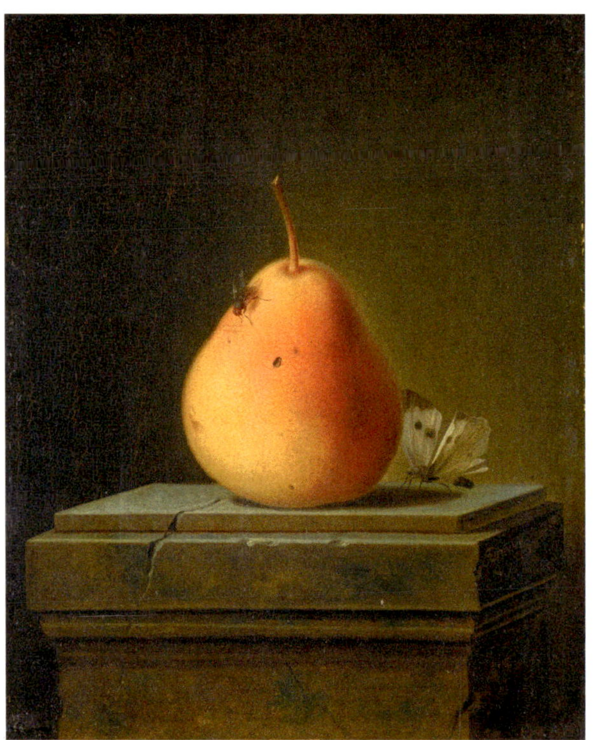

**9**   Justus Juncker, *Stillleben mit Birne und Insekten* |
*Still Life with Pear and Insects*, 1765, Eichenholz | Oak,
25,8 × 21,4 cm, Städel Museum, Frankfurt/M.

tropfte oder geworfene Klecks auf der Leinwand galt im „Dad Painting" als ungezügelter Ausdruck eines expressiven Aktes, der durch die getrocknete Form eine sichtbare Spur nach sich zog. Seit Hans Hartung in abstrakter und Francis Bacon in gegenständlicher Malerei wird der Klecks auch kalkuliert als Formelement eingesetzt. Im Zuge der oben erwähnten Erforschung basaler künstlerischer Mittel in der zeitgenössischen Malerei ist zur Zeit eine Rückkehr des Klecks oder Farbnebels als ironischer Kommentar des intuitiven Malgestus der Aktionsmalerei der 50er- und 60er-Jahre zu beobachten. Bemerkenswert ist allerdings, dass der Klecks nicht in den Kontext abstrakter, sondern gegenständlicher Malerei integriert wird. Als eine der bildnerischen Quellen fungiert wieder der Comic, der sich auch mit Buchs Arbeiten verbindet.

Von 2006 bis 2008 ist eine Beschleunigung des Ausbruchs der Farbmaterie aus dem Formgefüge in Buchs ikonischen Werken zu beobachten. Während die *Vase* von 2006 noch fast keine aktionistischen Spuren zeigt, platzen die Blütenformen der *Vase* von 2006 auf (Abb. S. 56/57). Auch die Farben in der *Matratze*, 2006, und im *Sofa*, 2007, beginnen sich am Linienrand, dann auch als Farbnebel im *Schuh*, 2006, zu verselbstständigen (Abb. S. 15). In den *Doppelmatratzen* von 2008 (Abb. S. 38/39) legen die Farbspuren ein filigranes Gespinst an Fäden, Klecksen und Tropfen über das Motiv. Die gänzliche Verflüssigung der Form in Farbmaterie scheint unmittelbar bevorzustehen. Damit wird nicht nur die prekäre Balance zwischen der Oberflächenstruktur des Gesamtbildes und der Oberfläche der dargestellten Objekte erheblich gestört, sondern auch das Scheitern ihrer ikonenhaften Ausstrahlung inszeniert. Die sichtbare Stofflichkeit holt das Objekt gewissermaßen wieder zu seinen Ursprüngen zurück.

Künstler wie Blaise Drummond (geb. 1967), Robert Sherratt (geb. 1970) oder Klaus-Martin Treder (geb. 1961; Abb. 10) haben begonnen, den Klecks als konzeptuelles Formelement bewusst einzusetzen, ihn zu simulieren, abzufotografieren, aus bestehenden Leinwänden herauszuoperieren und als Collageelement wieder auf die Leinwand zurückzuholen. Kleckse übernehmen plötzlich eine im bildnerischen Zusammenhang vielseitige Rolle und werden, wie bei Paul Cézanne die farbigen „tâches" (Flecken), als vieldeutige Naturäquivalente, u. a. auch als Insekt, eingesetzt.[26] Die künstlerische Praxis des sichtbaren Malprozesses, insbesondere des sogenannten Spontangestus, wird dabei neu definiert und ironisiert. In Abwandlung eines Zitats des

## Calculated unpredictability: The drip

In traditional still life painting a bu tterfly is frequently seen fluttering above the vegetables arranged on the table or a fly is seen sitting on the fruit (ill. 9). The insects not only suggest the transience of the depicted fruit, they also render visible the authenticity and thereby the finesse of the painting. In contemporary art the fluid and dripping colour materials take the place of the moving fly. In "Bad Painting", the splash dropped or thrown onto the canvas was considered as the unbridled expression of an expressive act that left a visible trace through the dry paint. Subsequent to the abstract painting of Hans Hartung and the figurative art of Francis Bacon, the drip has also become deliberately deployed as an element of form. In the course of the above mentioned examination of fundamental artistic methods within contemporary art it is possible to observe a current comeback on the part of the drip or the intensely dotted paint mist in the form of an ironic comment on the intuitive gestures of the Action Painting of the 50s and 60s. What is remarkable though is that the splotch is being integrated, not in the context of abstract, but of figurative painting. The comic-strip is once again a source of creativity and is also associated with Buch's work.

Between 2006 and 2008 Buch's iconic works show an escalation in the eruption of colour material out of the framework of the form. While the *Vase* from 2006 still bears no actionist traces (ill. p. 21), the forms of the blossom in the *Vase* from 2006 (ill. p. 56/57) are exploding. The colours in the *Double-mattress,* 2006 and in *Sofa,* 2007, are also beginning to break free at the edge of the line and then also as a mist of paint in *Shoe,* 2006 (ill. p. 15). In the *Double-mattresses* from 2008 (ill. p. 38/39), the traces of paint lay a delicate web of threads, splashes and drops across the motif. It would seem that the form will soon be turned entirely into fluid colour matter. As a result, not only is the precarious balance between the surface structure of the painting as a whole and the surface of the object portrayed considerably disrupted, but the failure of its iconic presence is also orchestrated. To a certain extent, the visible materiality returns the object to its fundamental origins again.

Artists such as Blaise Drummond (b. 1967), Robert Sherrat (b. 1970) and Klaus-Martin Treder (b. 1961; ill. 10) have begun to consciously introduce the drip as a conceptual component of

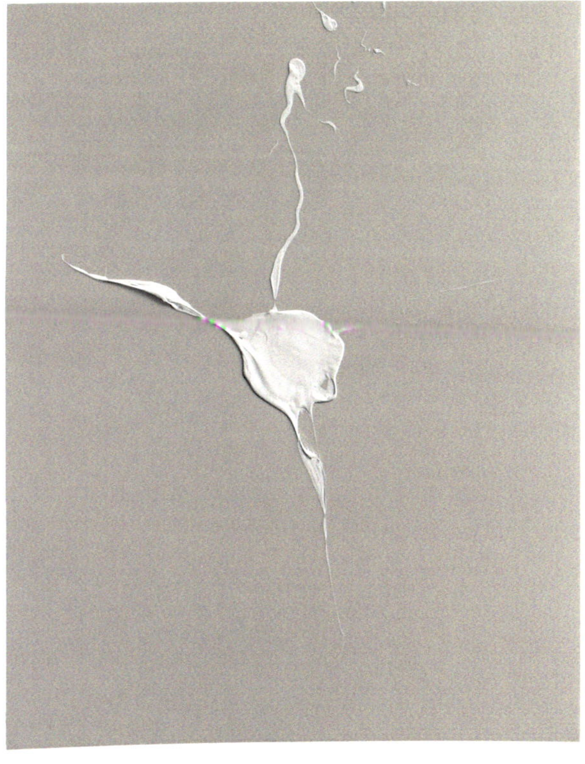

**10**  Klaus-Martin Treder, *Plakat Poster 04,* 2006, 97 × 68 cm (Tropfen. Versuchsreihe zur Viskosität der Farbe | Dripping. Series of Experiments on the Viscosity of Colour), Rede | Speech: Harald Braun. Im Besitz des Künstlers | Courtesy of the artist

Kunsthistorikers Gottfried Boehm könnte man sagen: Es ist der *kalkulierte* Möglichkeitssinn des Künstlers, auf den sich heute sein Wirklichkeitssinn stützt.[27] Denn mit den objektivierten Elementen kontrollierter Aktionsmalerei wird ein vorher nicht dagewesenes Kalkül eingeführt. Deshalb stehen diese Versuche der Pop-Art-Malerei eines Roy Lichtenstein wohl näher als die eines Jackson Pollock.

Morten Buchs Werke bewegen sich virtuos zwischen der Objektseligkeit der Pop-Art-Malerei und gestischer Abstraktion, formaler Perfektion und spontaner malerischer Gestik, zwischen dem absoluten Ding und einem Diskurs über Malerei überhaupt. Ist die Dingdarstellung etwa die letzte künstlerische Bastion geworden, um die Grundlagenforschung von Malerei voranzutreiben? In der stillgelegten Beschaulichkeit solider Dinge steckt nur scheinbar das Gegenteil von bildnerischer Kontingenz, vom „Möglichkeitssinn": Das Bild bewegt das Auge; der Betrachter ist IM Bild, während er das Bild betrachtet. Das Medium der Malerei ist bei Buch nicht nur künstlerische Erkenntniswerkstatt, eine Auseinandersetzung mit vertrauten Vorstellungen und deren Infragestellung, sondern auch die Ins-Bild-Setzung eines malerischen Anspruchs – den der *körperlichen* Rückversicherung. Der Titel der Ausstellung *The Last Resort* (Letzte Zuflucht) ist somit doppeldeutig zu verstehen: im räumlichen Sinn als das Aufsuchen eines Refugiums, in dem sich die Maler verschanzen, oder eben auch als hegemonialer Triumphzug des malerischen Aktes, der *peinture*, über alle anderen gegenwärtigen Medien wie Film, Fotografie und Internet, um deren eigenständige Möglichkeiten zu inszenieren.

form, to simulate it, to take photographs of it, to excise it out of existing canvases, restoring it again as an element of collage on the canvas. All of a sudden, splashes are taking on a versatile role in the creative context and becoming, as with the "tâches" (colour patches) of Paul Cézanne, employed as ambiguous substitutes to nature, amongst other things, also as insects.[26] The artistic practice of the visual painting process, in particular the so-called spontaneous gesture, is thus redefined and treated with irony.

Adapting a quotation from the art historian Gottfried Boehm, one could say that it is the artist's *deliberate* sense of possibility upon which today his sense of reality rests.[27] Through the objectivised elements of controlled action painting a degree of intentionality previously absent is introduced. These attempts are therefore possibly closer to the pop art painting of the likes of Roy Lichtenstein than they are to the likes of Jackson Pollock.

Morten Buch's works move skilfully between pop art's celebration of objects and gestural abstraction, formal perfection and spontaneous artistic gestures, between the thing as an absolute and a discourse on painting in general. Has the representation of the thing become something like the last artistic bastion with which to advance fundamental research in relation to painting? It is only on the face of it that the disappearance of tranquillity from solid things embodies the opposite of creative contingency, the sense of possibility: the painting moves the eye; the observer is IN the painting while he looks at it. In Buch's works, the medium of painting is not merely a workshop on art appreciation, a confrontation with familiar concepts, or, as the case may be, perceptions, with an attempt to challenge these, it is also the placing within the painting of an artistic aspiration – that of *physical* reassurance. Thus the title of the exhibition *The Last Resort* can be understood on two levels: in the spatial sense as the quest for a place of sanctuary where the artists entrench themselves, or indeed as the hegemonic victory parade of the creative act, the *peinture,* the triumph over all other contemporary media such as film, photography and the internet; the staging of its own possibilities.

1    Tal Rs Ansatz wird von Anders Kold mit dem Begriff „method painting" beschrieben. In: *The Sum. Tal R*, Ausst.-Kat. Louisiana Museum of Art, Humlebæk 2008, S. 17.

2    In ihrer einflussreichen dreiteiligen Ausstellungsreihe *Stop for a Moment – Painting as Presence / Painting as a Place to Be / Painting as Narrative* von 2002/03 stellten die Kuratoren Mika Hannula und Kari Immonen die Grundlagendiskussion zeitgenössischer Malerei ins Zentrum. Dabei mussten sie sich gegen den Vorwurf wehren, dass die skandinavischen Maler, darunter Tal R, Robert Lucander, John Kørner und Marcus Eek, zu sehr dem Malstil der 8oer-Jahren verpflichtet seien: „Many of the artists in the exhibition have been linked to the neo-expressive tradition of the 1980s German scene. Luckily these claims are unfounded. Artist's attitudes, values and opinions concerning their role and the status of painting could not be more opposed to the earnest pathos of the Neue Wilde … today's painters look critically at their practice and can even afford an occasional joke", siehe Nordic Institute for Contemporary Art, www.nifca.org/stopforamoment/press/press.html.

3    *Direkte Malerei* (Direct Painting) war der Titel einer Ausstellung in der Kunsthalle Mannheim 2005.

4    Troels Wörsel, „Notes on Painting. A Philosophical Negative" (1986), in: *Troels Wörsel*, Ausst.-Kat. The Nordic Watercolour Museum 2006, S. 22 (Hervorheb. von TW).

5    Margrit Rowell, *The Modern Still Life. Objects of Desire*, Ausst.-Kat. Museum of Modern Art, New York 1997, S. 125.

6    „Konzeptuelle Momente verbinden sich leichter mit Figurenbild und Stilleben (auch bei Cézanne)", in: Gottfried Boehm, *Paul Cézanne. Montagne Sainte-Victoire*, 1988, S. 124.

7    Luc Tuymans: „In *Still-Life* the idea of banality becomes larger than life, it's taken to an impossible extreme", in: „Interview with Julian Heynen", *Luc Tuymans*, Ausst.-Kat. Tate, London 2004, S. 9.

8    Sichtbar wird diese Tendenz beispielsweise im Hyperrealismus zeitgenössischer Malerei, in der Rückkehr zum Handwerk in der heutigen Designbranche, deren Produkte auf den Produktionsprozess verweisen oder der aktuellen Werbekampagne des Wolfsburger VW-Autokonzerns, die dem Kunden den VW-Wagen als „DAS Auto" präsentiert.

9    Korff, in: *Zeitschrift für Kulturwissenschaften*, hrsg. von Michael C. Frank et al., „Fremde Dinge", Bielefeld, Nr. 1/2007, S. 32.

10    Martin Heidegger, *Der Ursprung des Kunstwerkes*, Stuttgart 1960, S. 25.

11    Das Motiv des Zeltes verwendeten beispielsweise auch Vanessa Bell, Markus Lüpertz und Miriam Bäckström. Der Schuh tritt bei van Gogh, Andy Warhol, Roy Lichtenstein und Philip Guston auf. Die Matratze erhält eine zentrale Rolle bei Francis Bacon und Dieter Krieg.

12    Morten Buch 2003, in: *Morten Buch*, Katalog Galleri Susanne Ottesen, Kopenhagen 2003, S. 22.

13    Idem.

14    Martin Heidegger (siehe Anm. 10), S. 26: „Das Zeugsein des Zeugs besteht in seiner Dienlichkeit".

15    Bruno Latour, in: *Zeitschrift für Kulturwissenschaften* (siehe Anm. 9), S. 65.

16    So Buch und Jensen im Gespräch 2001: „But at the same time, we've also aspired toward a textural quality and a sensuality – a carnality – and this is all connected with a certain identification with the very object of the picture", in: *Take off 20:01*, Ausst.-Kat. Kunstmuseum Aarhus 2001, n. p.

17    Maurice Merleau-Ponty, in: *Das Sichtbare und das Unsichtbare*, München 1994, S. 15.

18    Bettina Gockel, „Van Goghs Schuhe. Zum Streit zwischen Heidegger und Meyer Schapiro", in: *Zeitschrift für Kulturwissenschaften* (siehe Anm. 9), S. 88. Als weitere Referenzen für die Entstehung des Einzelmotivs seit 1850 sind zu nennen Henri Fantin-Latours *Weisse Tasse und Untertasse*, 1864, Öl auf Leinwand, 19,4 × 28,9 cm (Fitzwilliam Museum Cambridge) und Edouard Manets isolierte Darstellungen von Stillebenmotiven wie in *Spargel*, 1880, oder *Zitrone*, 1880/81, beide Öl auf Leinwand, 16 × 21 und 14 × 21 cm (Paris, Musée d'Orsay).

19    Kazimir Malewitsch, *Die gegenstandslose Welt*, Erstausgabe aus dem Manuskript übers. von Alexander von Riesen, München 1927, S. 74: „Das schwarze Quadrat auf dem weißen Feld war die erste Ausdrucksform der gegenstandslosen Empfindung: das Quadrat = die Empfindung, das weiße Feld = das ‚Nichts' außerhalb dieser Empfindung."

20    So lautet der erste Titel auf Trentemøllers CD *The Last Resort* (2006), die dem vorliegenden Katalog und der Ausstellung den Namen gegeben hat.

21    Maurice Merleau-Ponty (siehe Anm. 17), S. 331.

22    Martin Heidegger (siehe Anm. 10), S. 17.

23    Maurice Merleau-Ponty (siehe Anm. 17), S. 191.

24    Wenn Delacroix' Palette als „kostbarer Blumenstrauß", van Goghs als „Feldstrauß" charakterisiert wurde, dann sind die Farben von Buchs Palette aus der heutigen Designbranche geborgt.

25    Georges Didi-Huberman, in: *Die leibhaftige Malerei (La peinture incarnée)*, aus dem Franz. übers. von Michael Wetzel, München 2002, S. 40–41.

26    Blaise Drummond: „I always use them [die Kleckse, vw] to generate and stand in for organic elements – trees, plants, leaves, insects … those sort of things", in: *Blaise Drummond. By The Shores of Lake Eden*, Ausst.-Kat. Rubicon Gallery, Dublin 2005, n. p.

27    Gottfried Boehms Originalzitat lautet: „Mit Musils Unterscheidung darf man auch sagen: es ist der Möglichkeitssinn des Künstlers, auf den sich sein Wirklichkeitssinn stützt", in: Gottfried Boehm (siehe Anm. 6), S. 59.

**1**  Anders Kold uses the term "method painting" to describe Tal R's approach. In: *The Sum. Tal R,* Exhibition Catalogue, Louisiana Museum of Art, Humlebæk 2008, p. 17.

**2**  The curators Mika Hannula and Kari Immonen placed the fundamental debate on contemporary painting at the centre of their influential three-part exhibition series *Stop for a Moment – Painting as Presence / Painting as a Place to Be / Painting as Narrative* from 2002/03. In the process, they had to counter the claim that the Scandanavian painters, including Tal R, Robert Lucander, John Kørner and Marcus Eek owed too much to the style of painting of the 1980s: "Many of the artists in the exhibition have been linked to the neo-expressive tradition of the 1980s German scene. Luckily these claims are unfounded. Artists' attitudes, values and opinions concerning their role and the status of painting could not be more opposed to the earnest pathos of the Neue Wilde … today's painters look critically at their practice and can even afford an occasional joke", see homepage of Nordic Institute of Contemporary Art, www.nifca. org/stopforamoment/press/press.html.

**3**  *Direkte Malerei* (Direct Painting) was the title of an exhibition at Kunsthalle Mannheim 2005.

**4**  Troels Wörsel: "Notes on Painting. A Philosophical Negative" (1986), in: *Troels Worsel,* Exhibition Catalogue, The Nordic Watercolour Museum, 2006, p. 22 (emphasis by TW).

**5**  Margrit Rowell, *The Modern Still Life. Objects of Desire,* Exhibition Catalogue, Museum of Modern Art, New York 1997, p. 125.

**6**  "Conceptual motives are more readily associated with figure paintings and still lifes (this is also the case with Cézanne)." Gottfried Boehm, *Paul Cézanne. Montagne Sainte-Victoire,* Frankfurt/M. 1988, p. 124.*

**7**  Luc Tuymans: „In *Still-Life* the idea of banality becomes larger than life, it's taken to an impossible extreme", in: "Interview with Julian Heynen", *Luc Tuymans,* Exhibition Catalogue, Tate, London 2004, p. 9.

**8**  This tendency becomes apparent for instance in the Hyper Realism of contemporary painting, in the re-emergence of craftsmanship in today's design industry where products are indicative of the production process, and in the current advertising campagne of the VW corporation in Wolfsburg where the VW is presented to the customer as "THE Car".

**9**  Korff, in: *Zeitschrift für Kulturwissenschaften,* ed. Michael C. Frank et al., "Fremde Dinge" ("Foreign things"), Bielefeld, Nr. 1/2007, p. 32.*

**10**  Martin Heidegger, *Der Ursprung des Kunstwerkes,* Stuttgart 1960, p. 25.*

**11**  The motif of the tent was also made use of by, for instance, Vanessa Bell, Markus Lüpertz and Miriam Bäckström. The shoe appears in the works of Van Gogh, Andy Warhol, Roy Lichtenstein and Philip Guston. The mattress acquires a central role in the works of Francis Bacon and Dieter Krieg.

**12**  Morten Buch 2003, in: *Morten Buch,* Catalogue Galleri Susanne Ottesen, Copenhagen 2003, p. 22.

**13**  Ibid.

**14**  Martin Heidegger (see quote 10), p. 20 ff. und p. 26: „Das Zeugsein des Zeugs besteht in seiner Dienlichkeit" ("The 'implemental being' of the implement lies in its usefulness").*

**15**  Bruno Latour, in: *Zeitschrift für Kulturwissenschaften* (see quote 9), p. 65.

**16**  According to Buch und Jensen 2001: "But at the same time, we've also aspired towards a textural quality and a sensuality – a carnality – and this is all connected with a certain identification with the very object of the picture." In: *Take off* 20:01, Exhibition Catalogue, Kunstmuseum Aarhus 2001, n. p.

**17**  Maurice Merleau-Ponty in: *Das Sichtbare und das Unsichtbare,* München 1994, p. 15.*

**18**  Bettina Gockel, "Van Goghs Schuhe. Zum Streit zwischen Heidegger und Meyer Schapiro", in: *Zeitschrift für Kulturwissenschaften* (see quote 9), p. 88. See also: Henri Fantin-Latours *White Cup and Saucer* 1864, oil on canvas, 19,4 × 28,9 cm (Fitzwilliam Museum Cambridge) und Edouard Manet's representation of an *Asparagus,* 1880, or a *Lemon,* 1880/81, both oil on canvas, 16 × 21 und 14 × 21 cm (Paris, Musée d'Orsay).

**19**  Kazimir Malewitsch, *Die gegenstandslose Welt,* First edition from the manuscript transl. by Alexander von Riesen, München 1927, p. 74: "Das schwarze Quadrat auf dem weißen Feld war die erste Ausdrucksform der gegenstandslosen Empfindung: das Quadrat = die Empfindung, das weiße Feld = das ‚Nichts' außerhalb dieser Empfindung." ("The black square on the white background was the first expression of non-objective sensation: the square = the sensation, the white background = the 'nothingness' outside of this sensation."*).

**20**  Title of the first track on Trentemøller's CD *The Last Resort* (2006) from which came the title of the present catalogue and exhibition.

**21**  Maurice Merleau-Ponty (see quote 17), p. 331.

**22**  Martin Heidegger (see quote 10), p. 17.

**23**  Maurice Merleau-Ponty (see quote 17), p. 191.*

**24**  If Delacroix's palette was described as a "sumptous bouquet" and van Gogh's as a "bunch of wild flowers", then the colours of Buch's palette seem borrowed from today's design industry.

**25**  Georges Didi-Huberman, in: *Die leibhaftige Malerei (La peinture incarnée),* translated from the French by Michael Wetzel, München 2002, p. 40–41.

**26**  Blaise Drummond: „I always use them [the drips, vw] to generate and stand in for organic elements – trees, plants, leaves, insects … those sort of things", in: *Blaise Drummond. By The Shores of Lake Eden,* Exhibition Catalogue, Rubicon Gallery, Dublin 2005, n. p.

**27**  The original quotation by Gottfried Boehm reads as follows: "With Musil's distinction, one might also say: it is the artist's sense of possibility upon which his sense of reality rests", in: Gottfried Boehm (see quote 9), p. 59.*

* Translated from German by Marisia Kucharski

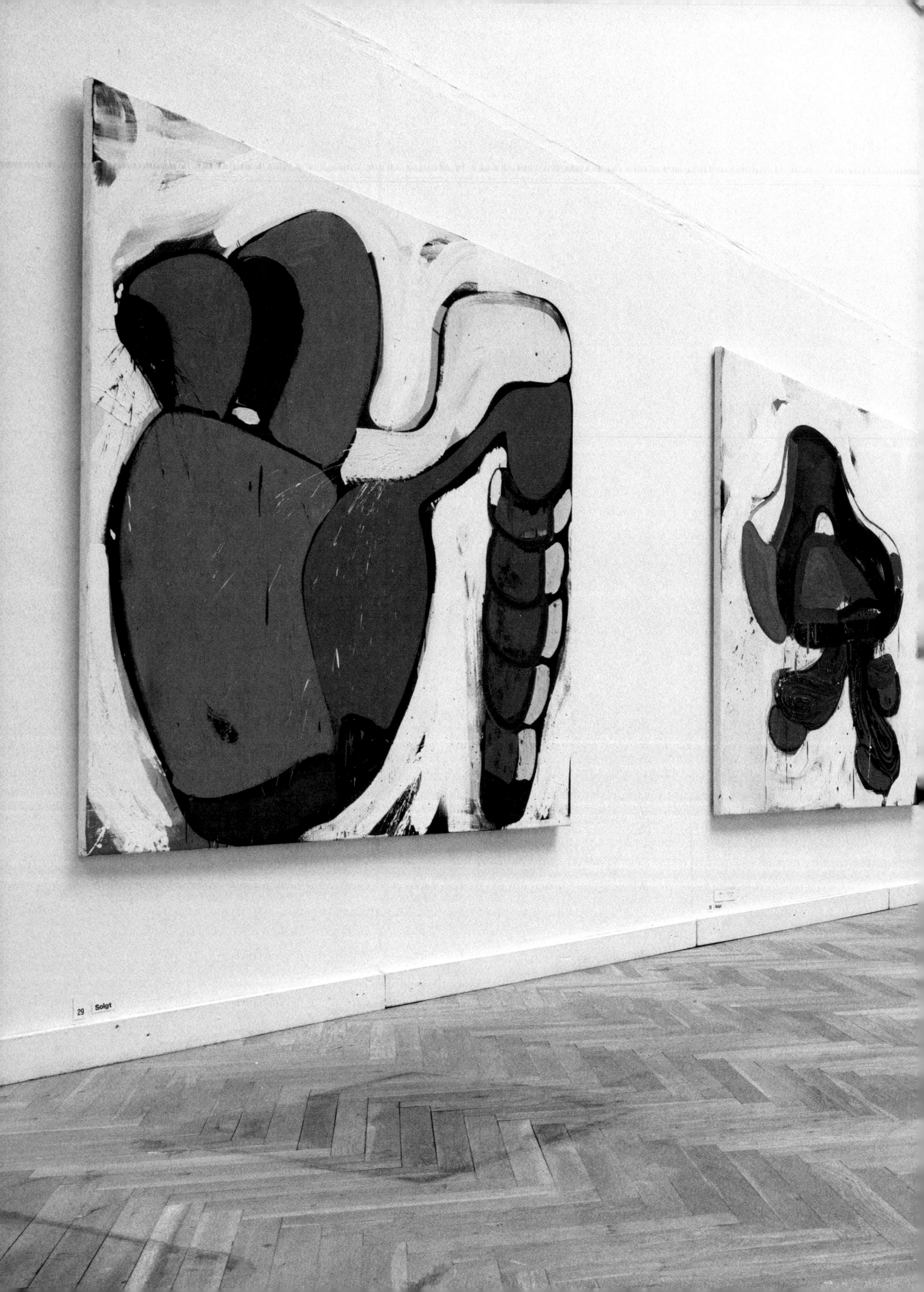

29 Solgt

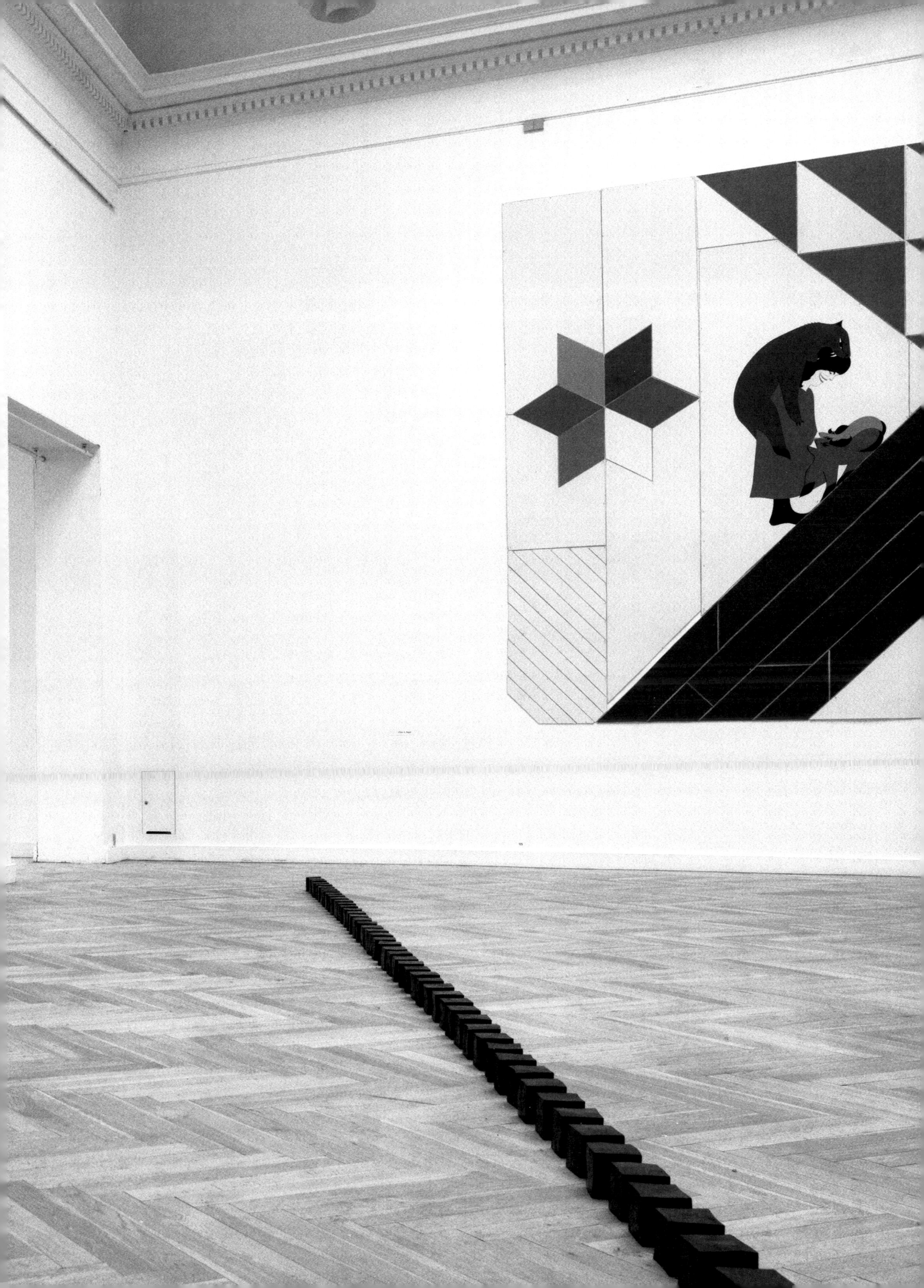

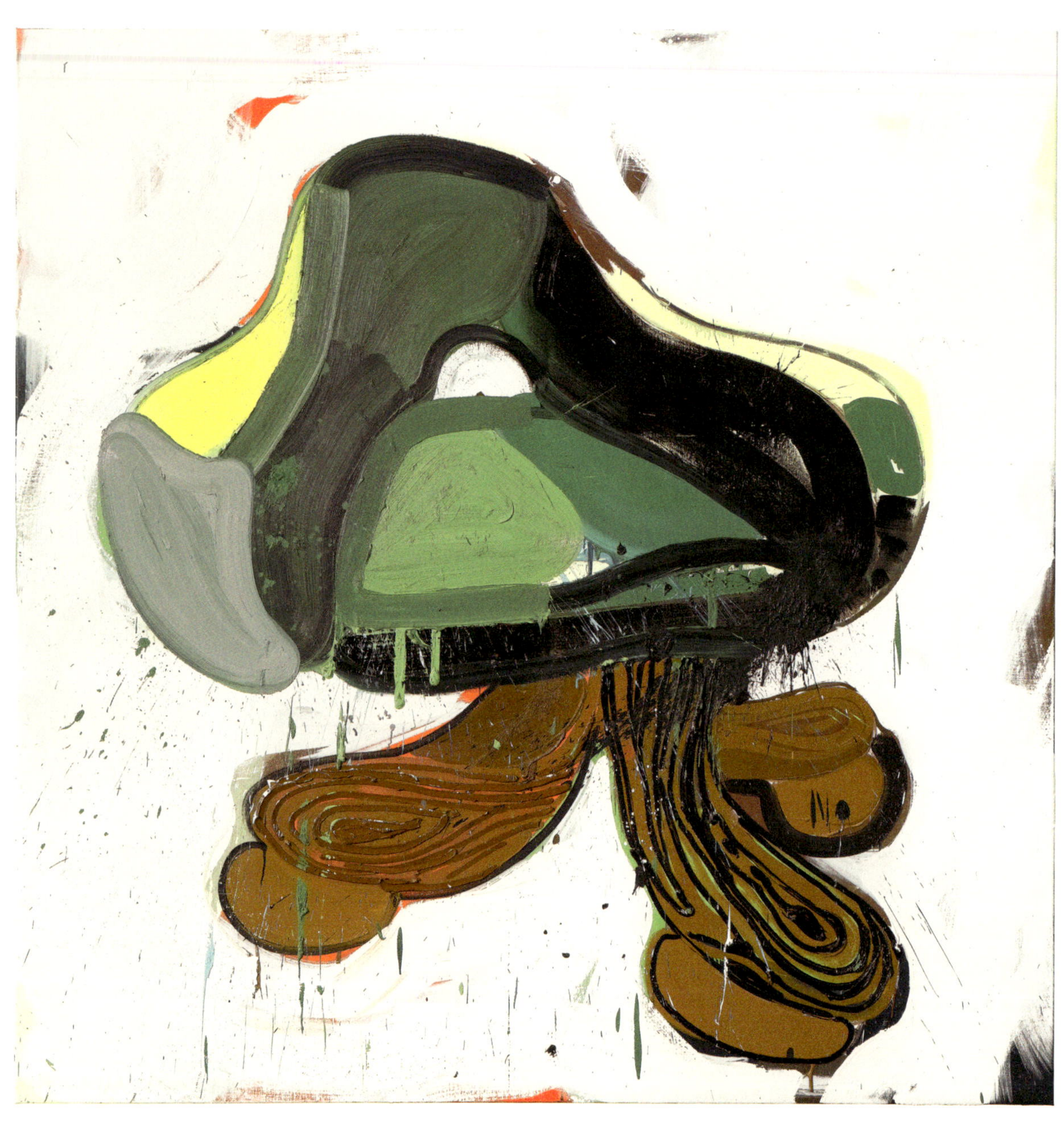



Stol 2006

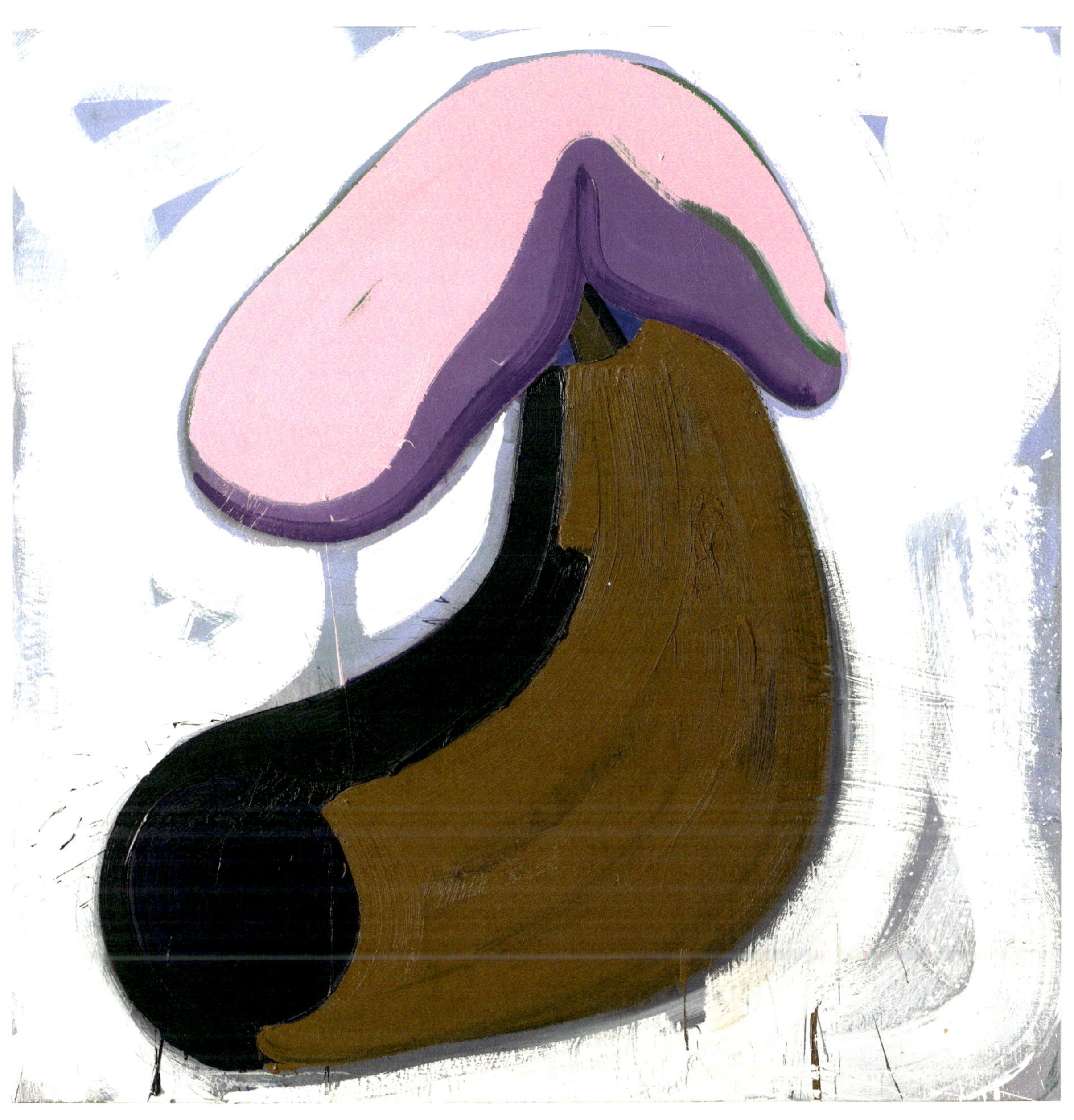

Vase 2008

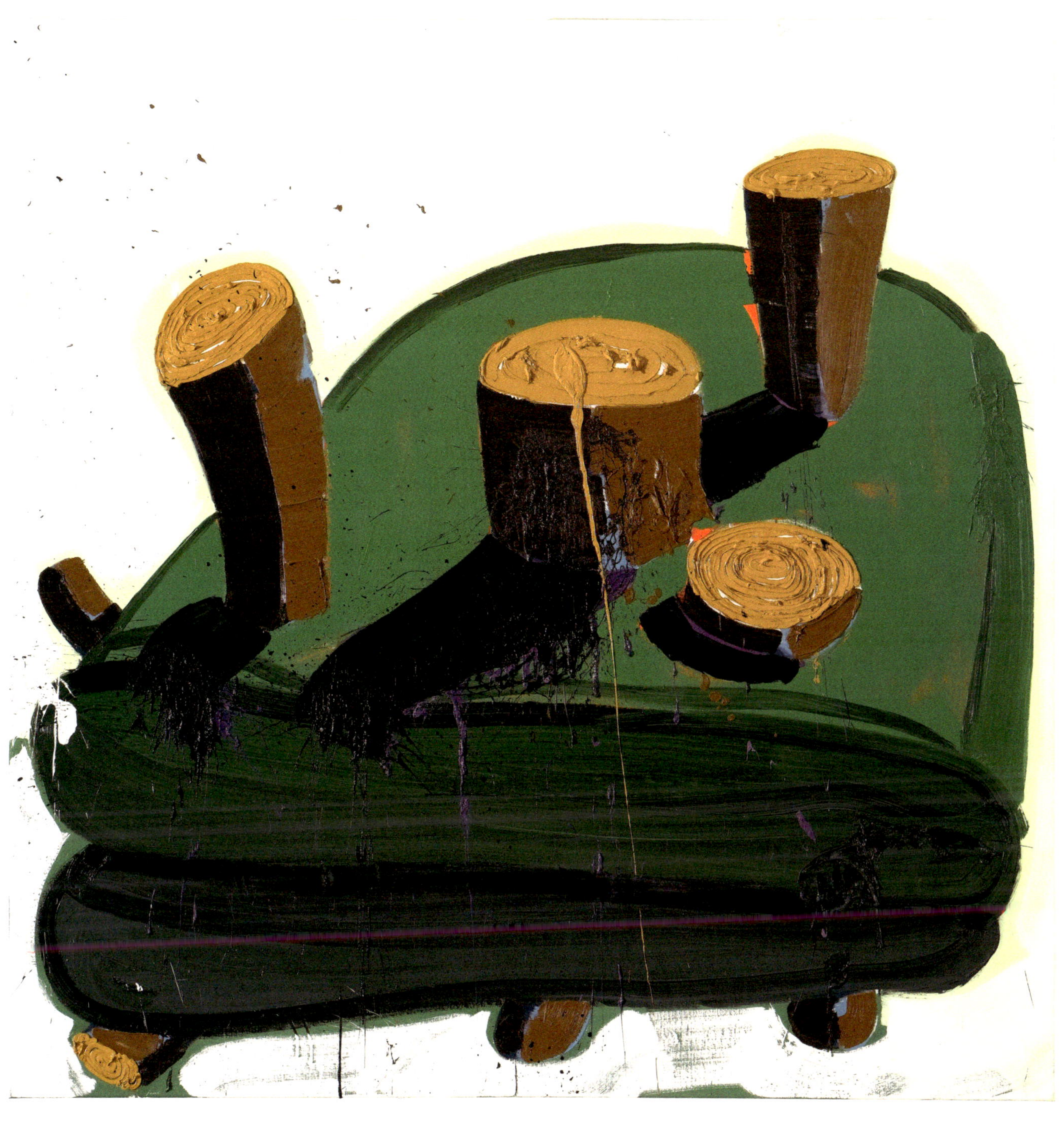

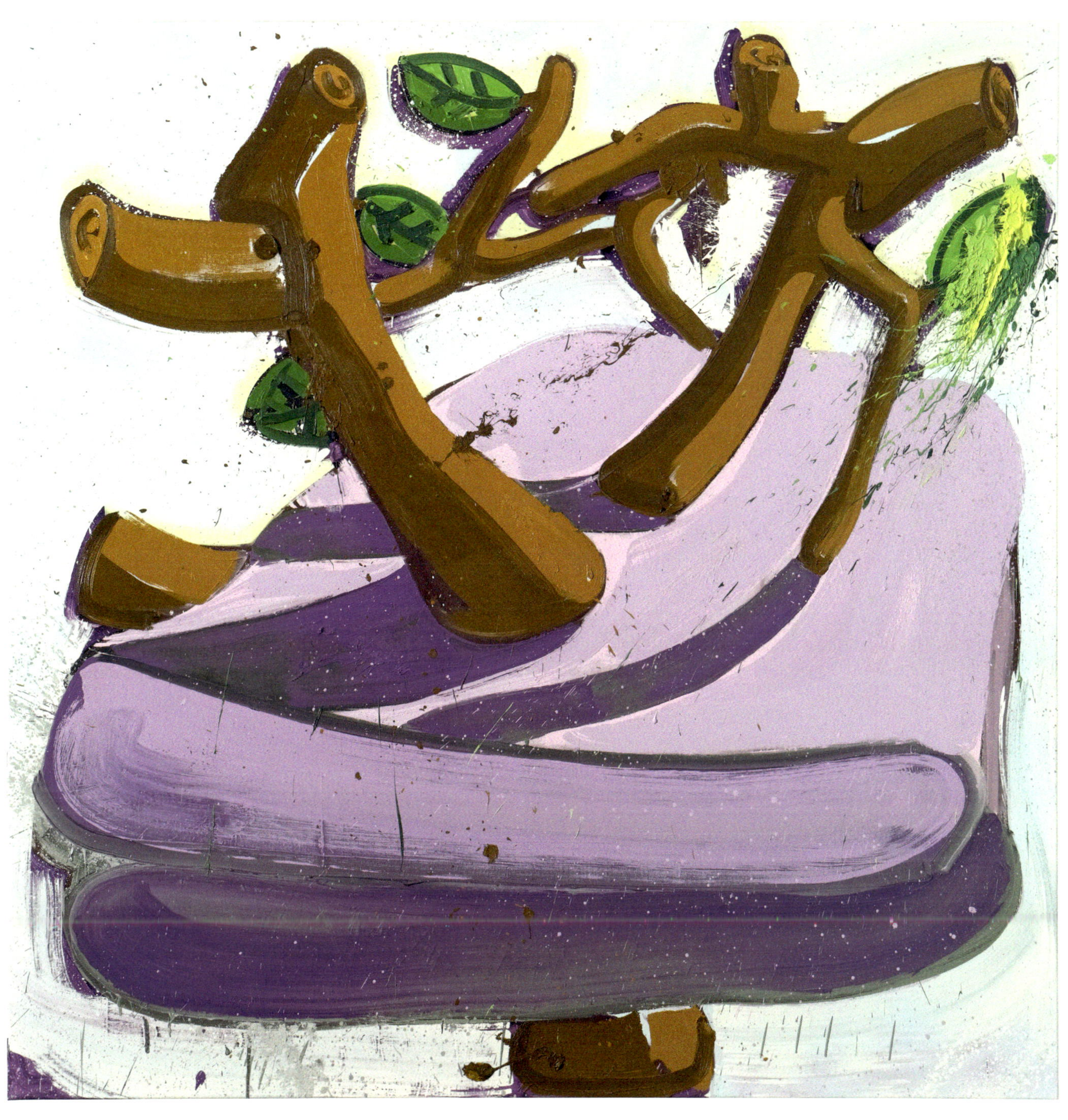

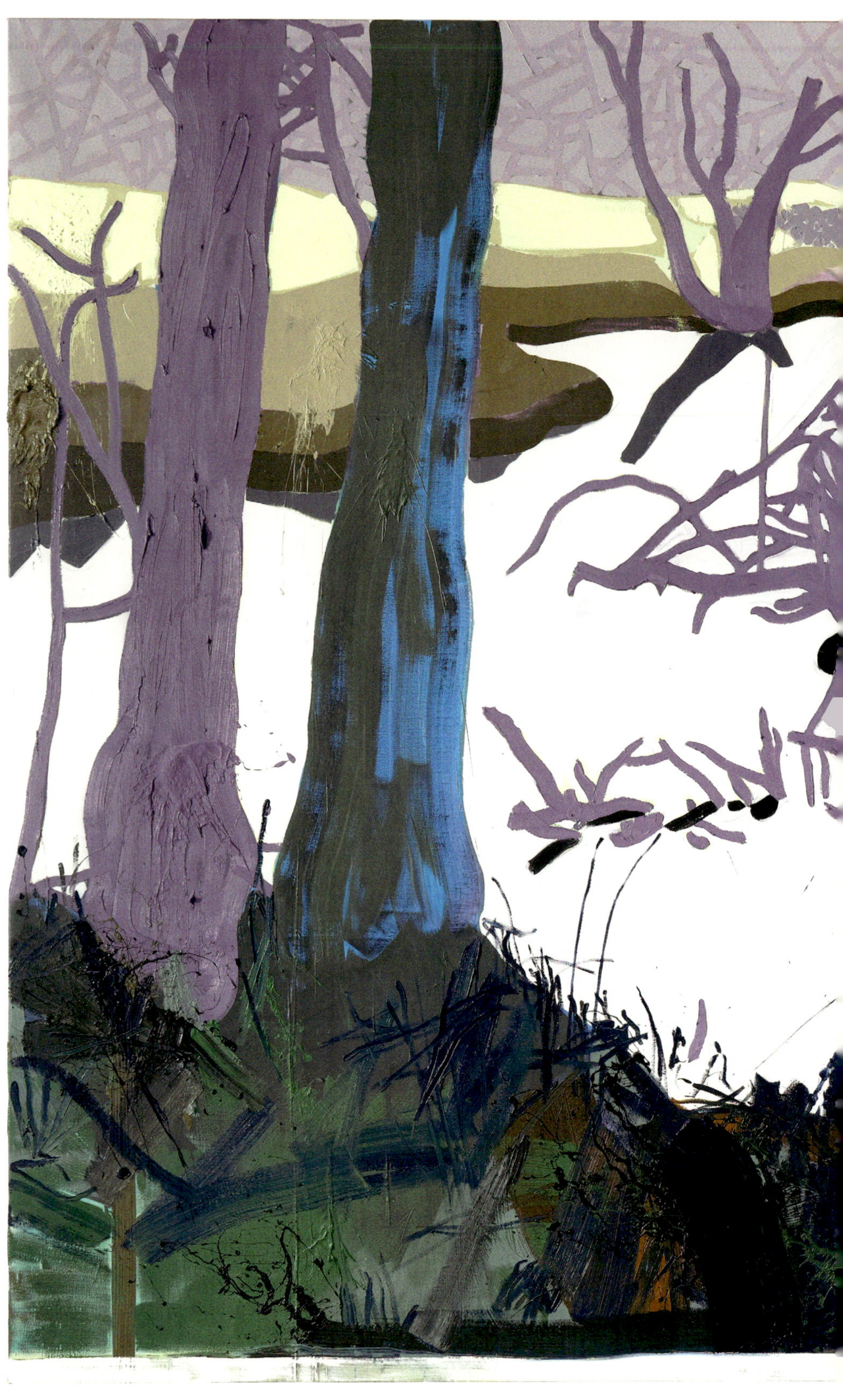

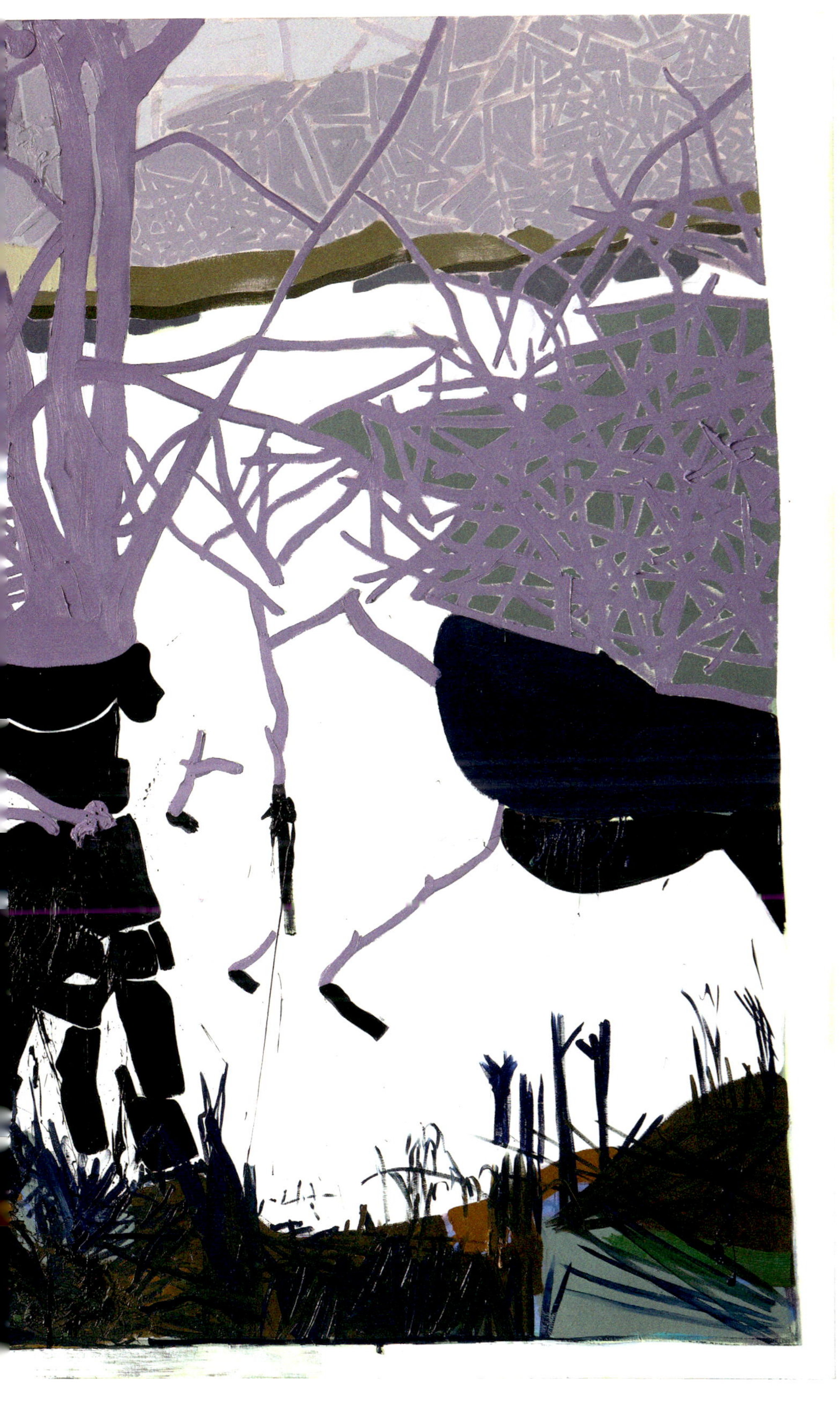

Landskab 2008

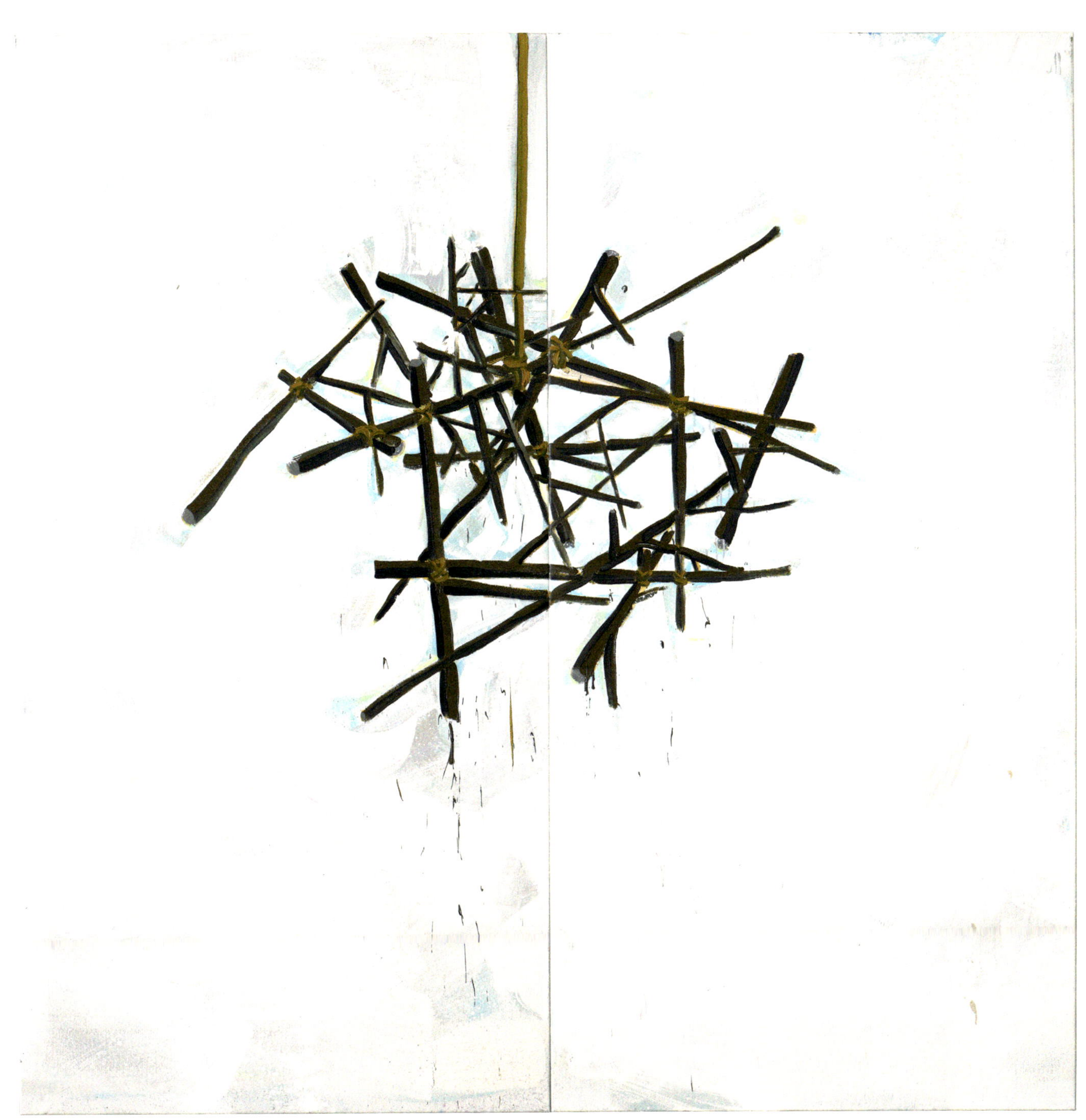

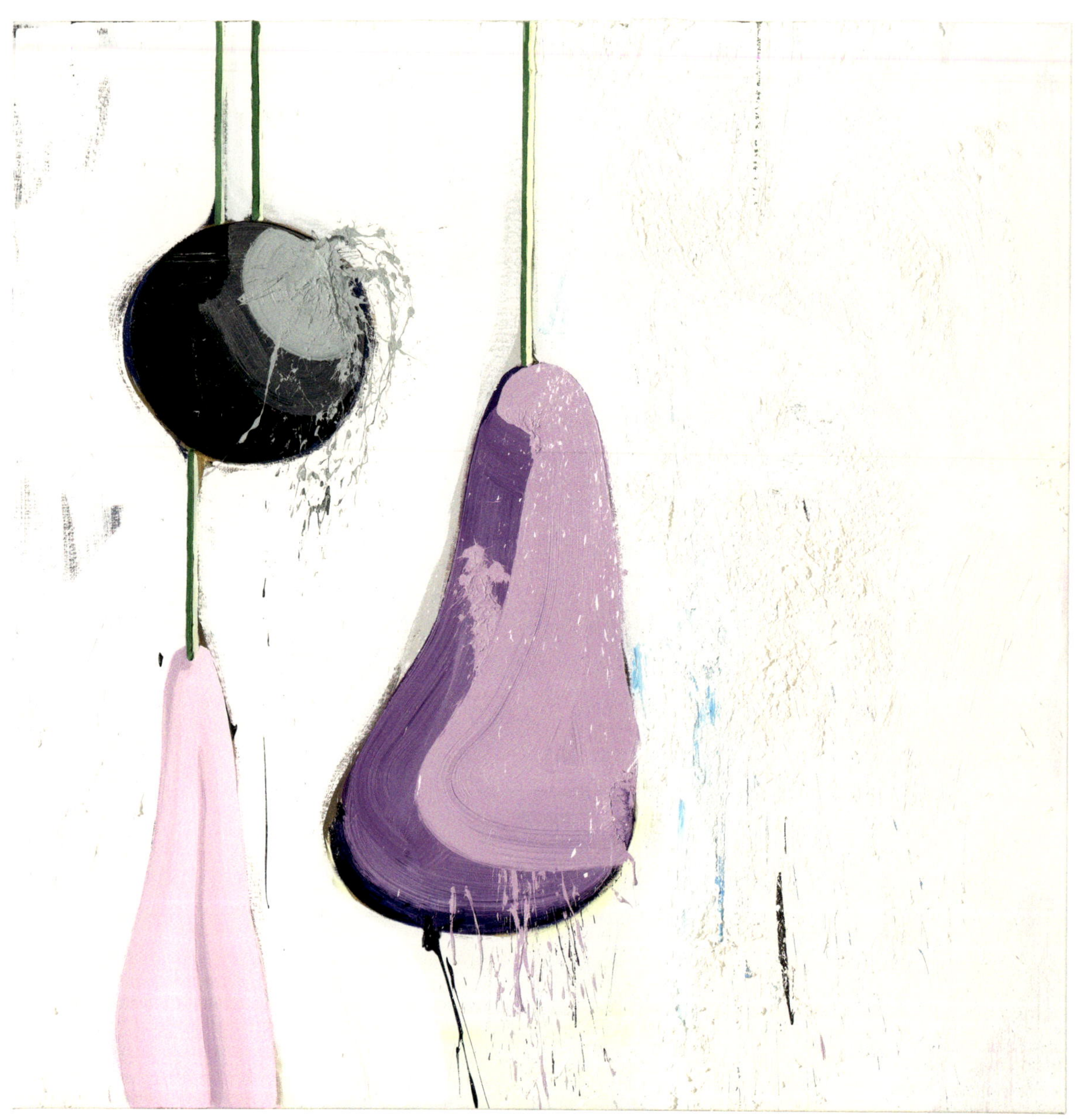



**Stilleben** 2007

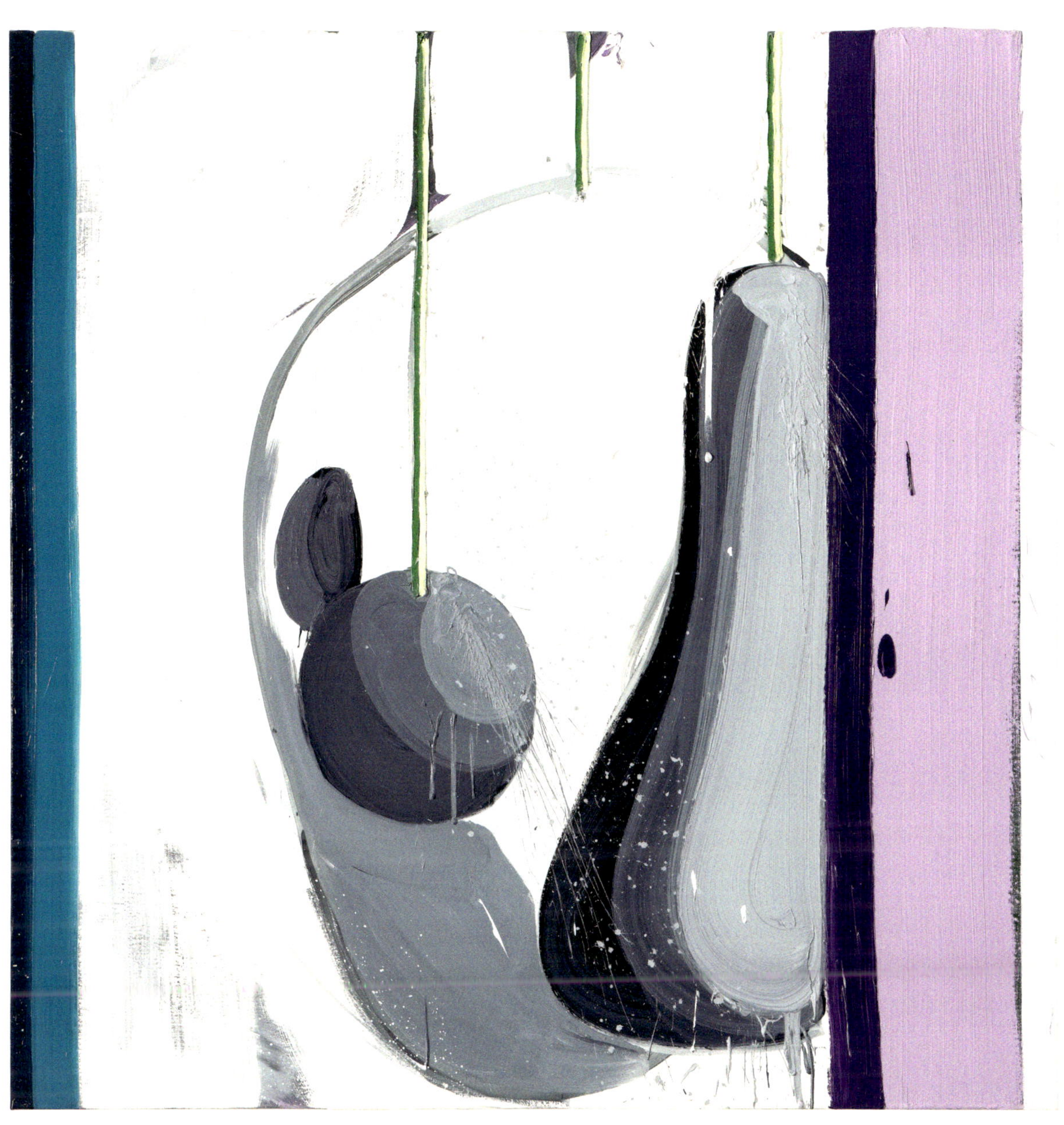

**Stilleben** 2007

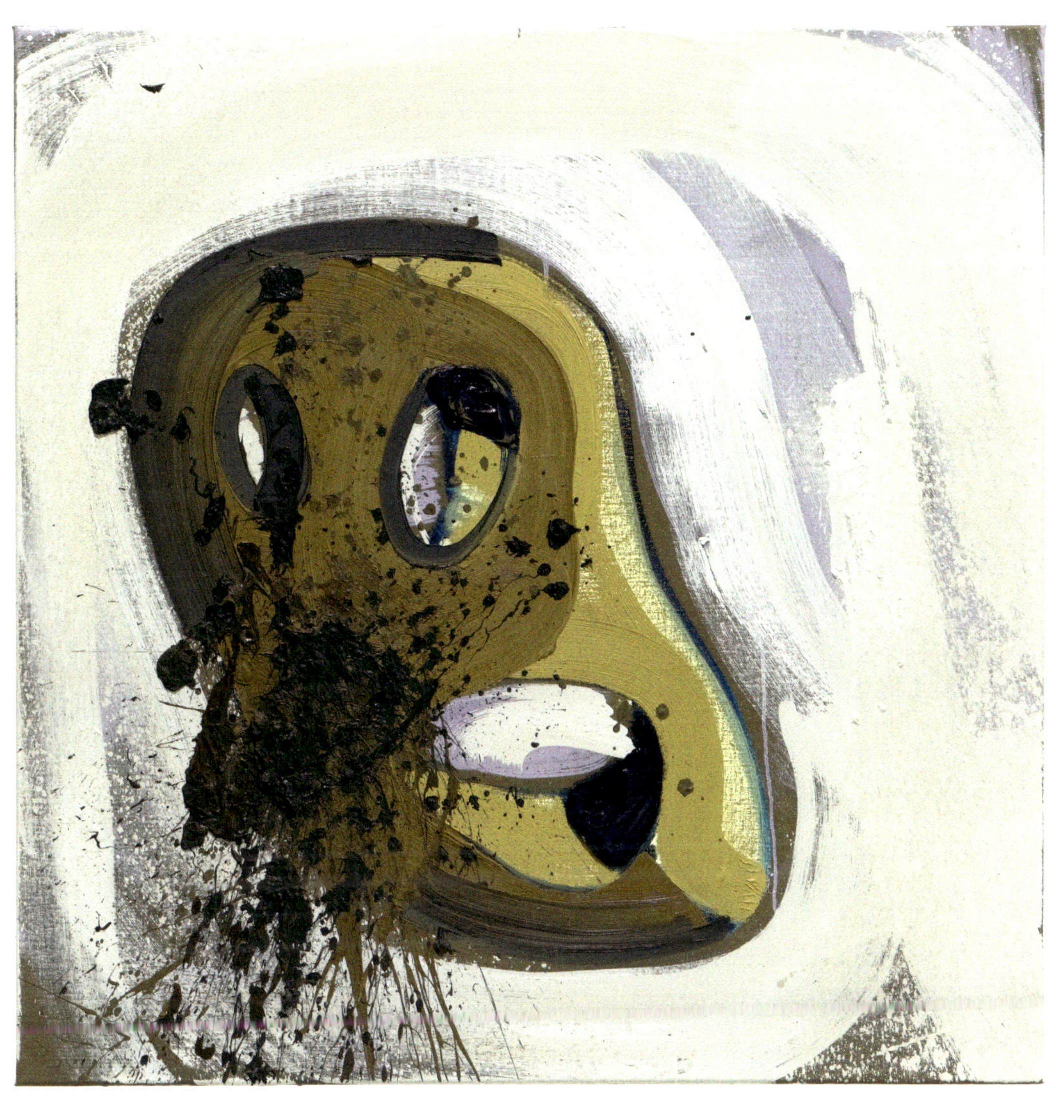

Uden Titel  2007

<h1 style="color:#c8d700">Interview mit</h1>

von Maibritt Pedersen

Platon meinte, dass zwar alle Pferde unterschiedlich seien, aber alle aus derselben Form gegossen – aus der Form „Pferd", die dazu führt, dass wir alle ein Pferd als solches erkennen, wenn wir es sehen. Die reine Form, die Grundform eines Objektes, ist gleichzeitig die dem Objekt innewohnende Idee und ihr innerstes Wesen. Morten Buchs (geb. 1970) aktuelle Ausstellung, *No Halo*, handelt davon, was passiert, wenn sich diese Form aus ihrer Grundbedeutung löst und damit das innerste Wesen der Dinge infrage stellt. Was geschieht mit uns Betrachtern, wenn wir auf eine Form treffen, die wir wiedererkennen, die aber gleichzeitig fremd auf uns wirkt? Die uns zwingt, Stellung zu beziehen zur Selbstverständlichkeit dieses Objekts, das einen Teil unserer Verankerung in der Welt ausmacht, und zu unserem Verhältnis zu den Dingen, die uns umgeben? Der Titel der Ausstellung – *Kein Heiligenschein* – bezieht sich auf den Wunsch, nicht nach einer Transzendierung der Motive im traditionellen Verständnis zu streben. Wenn kein Heiligenschein die Objekte krönt, wenn sie stattdessen verweltlicht werden, wird es erst möglich, ihre Form und ihre Nebenbedeutung herauszufordern – und so ein auf den ersten Blick selbstverständliches und leicht wiedererkennbares Motiv an ganz neue Orte zu verschieben.

*Als erster Eindruck, wenn man Ihre Ausstellung betrachtet, fällt einem auf, dass Sie durchgehend figurativ an Ihre Arbeiten herangehen und dafür leicht wiedererkennbare, alltägliche Motive wählen: eine Vase, ein Zelt, einen Schuh …*

Auch wenn einem das unmittelbar ins Auge fällt, ist die Wahl der Motive vielleicht nicht das Entscheidende. Es geht nicht so sehr darum, ob es dieses oder jenes ist. Was mich wirklich interessiert, sind die Assoziationen, die die Motivwahl hervorruft. Ein Motiv setzt den Betrachter rein psychologisch immer auf eine Fährte. Es berechtigt dazu, bestimmte Dinge mit Form und Farbe zu tun, die rein abstrakt nur schwer erreicht werden können. In abstrakter Malerei bleibt man häufig an einer Systematik hängen oder ganz an sich selbst. Mit einem Motiv kann man auf ganz andere Ideen kommen, neue Sachen machen und vielleicht auch die Farbe präziser auf die Leinwand auftragen. Die Farben können auf bestimmte Weise aufgeteilt werden, aber auch eher irrationale Dinge sind möglich. Es fängt damit an, dass man etwas sieht – ein Ding, eine Form –, das einen Eindruck hinterlässt und das man gerne wiedergeben möchte. Tatsächlich aber wird es dann etwas

ganz anderes. Es setzt sich in Bewegung und ändert den Charakter, wenn man mit dem Malen beginnt.

*Obwohl Ihre Bilder stets von der Wahl einer Gegenstandsdarstellung geprägt sind, vermitteln sie ebenso den Eindruck von tief empfundener Freude an Farbe und von dem Wissen über Farbe …*

Für mich sind die Textur und die Art und Weise, wie sich die Farbe auf der Leinwand verhält und verändert, genauso bedeutsam wie mein figurativer Zugang. Ich möchte eine bestimmte Intensität wiedergeben, ein bestimmtes visuelles Erlebnis, das in hohem Maße an die Farbe gekoppelt ist. Aber Textur und Ausdruck handeln meiner Meinung nach auch stark davon, dass das Auge sich auf eine bestimmte Art durch das Bild bewegen kann. In dieser Hinsicht weist diese Ausstellung auch zurück auf meine Erfahrungen als abstrakter Maler, als ich erforscht habe, was notwendig ist, damit ein Bild wirkt. In gewisser Weise profitiere ich heute von dieser Arbeit. Ich konstruiere meine Bilder möglichst solide – sowohl das Motiv, als auch den Untergrund und die verwendeten Farben –, sodass von meiner Warte aus nichts damit schiefgehen kann. Ich versuche, jedes Bild so perfekt zu komponieren, dass es auch dann noch gelänge, wenn mir irgendein schreckliches Missgeschick passierte – selbst wenn ich in die Leinwand fiele! Und ich setze sehr kalkulierte Effekte ein. Mit den Farben, die ich benutze, möchte ich gerne eine ganz bestimmte Wirkung erzielen. Sie sollen klar und präzise sein, und ich finde, Frank Stella hat das sehr genau formuliert, als er sagte, dass er sich gut vorstellen könne, dass die Farben auf der Leinwand so schön blieben wie sie im Farbtopf waren. Das halte ich für ein ganz wunderbares Bestreben, dass man die Farbe nicht zerstört, sondern demütig ist und versucht, ihre Qualität in der Verarbeitung zu erhalten.

*Obwohl Ihre Bilder so präzise und wohlüberlegt sind, strahlen sie auch eine Form von Grobheit, Wildheit und expressiver Energie aus …*

Das ist auch unglaublich wichtig, dass ein Bild ein „Jetzt" hat, dass es unmittelbar wirkt. Für mich erinnert Malerei an Theater – dieses Gefühl, dass es „live" ist, und dass es auch schiefgehen könnte. Darum ist es unglaublich wichtig, dass alle Striche exakt sitzen und auf ihre Positionierung im Werk aufmerksam machen. Man soll den Eindruck gewinnen, es hätte danebengehen können, sie hätten anders platziert werden können. Mir geht es selbst so, wenn ich fühle, dass der Ausdruck eines Gemäldes einen langwierigen und sorgfältig geplanten Prozess abbildet, dann fange ich

# with Morten Buch

by Maibritt Pedersen

According to Plato, although all horses are different, they are nevertheless all cast from the same mould – the form 'horse' – the form that allows us all to recognise a horse when we come across one. This pure form – the basic form of the object – is simultaneously the inherent conception and the innermost nature of the object. Morten Buch's (b. 1970) current exhibition, *No Halo,* is about what happens when this form divorces itself from its original meaning, thereby challenging its innermost nature. What happens to us when we encounter and observe a form we clearly recognise, but at the same time appears alien to us? A form that compels us to adopt a position both in relation to the given qualities of an object that is a constituent element of everything that anchors us in the world, and in relation to the way we relate to our surroundings? The title of the exhibition – *No Halo* – refers to the endeavour to avoid a transcendental rendering of the motifs in the traditional sense. With no halos and rendered objects of this world again, only then is it possible to challenge their form and their connotations – and so to relocate seemingly obvious and familiar motifs.

*What strikes one first about the exhibition is your consistently figurative approach and your choice of familiar and everyday motifs – a vase, a tent, a shoe …*

Even if this is what is most conspicuous at first, the choice of motif is not necessarily the key factor. It is not so much a question of it being one thing or another. Of real interest to me are the associations evoked by the choice of motif. A motif will, psychologically speaking, always lead the observer down a particular track.  It justifies doing certain things – in relation to form as well as colour – that are otherwise hard to achieve by purely abstract means. With abstract painting, you frequently become trapped in a particular system or completely caught up in yourself. With a motif, however, you can come up with quite different ideas, create something new and maybe even apply the colours with greater precision on the canvas. You can be quite intentional about how you distribute the colours, but other less rational things are possible too. You begin by seeing something – an object, a form – that makes an  impression on you, something that you want to depict. In actual fact, however, it then becomes something quite different. It is set in motion and its character changes when you begin to paint.

*Your paintings consistently reflect your decision to depict objects, and yet they also convey a deep love and knowledge of colour …*

The texture and the way the colour behaves and changes on the canvas are just as important to me as the figurative approach. I seek to convey a particular intensity, a certain visual experience that is closely linked to the colour. However, in my mind, texture and expressivity are also very much about the fact that the eye is able to rove across the painting in a particular way. In that sense, this exhibition also harks back to my earlier experiences as an abstract painter when I would explore what it took to make a painting work. In a way, I am able to reap the benefit of that work today. I try to structure my paintings – the motif as well as the colours I use – as much as possible so that, as far as I'm concerned, nothing can go wrong. I try to compose each painting so meticulously that if some awful accident were to occur – even if I were to go crashing into the painting – it would still turn out well. And the effects I introduce are highly calculated. The colours I use are intended to achieve a very specific impression. They must be bright and precise, and I think Frank Stella put it very well when he said that he envisaged the colours remaining as beautiful on the canvas as they were in the paint pot. I think this is a wonderful aspiration; not to spoil the colour, but be modest and attempt to maintain the quality of the colour as you work with it.

*Even though your paintings are so precise and so deliberate, they still radiate a kind of rawness, ferocity and expressive energy …*

It is also extremely important that the painting has a 'now', an immediacy. Painting reminds me of the theatre – that feeling that it is 'live' and that it could all go wrong. That is why it is incredibly important that each brush stroke falls in exactly the right place and draws attention to its positioning in the work. You should have an impression that it could have gone wrong, that they could have been placed differently. Personally, once I begin to feel that the expression of the painting testifies to a long and carefully planned process, I simply get bored. This does not necessarily make the painting any worse; I just find it unbearable.

einfach an, mich zu langweilen. Es macht das Bild eigentlich nicht
schlechter. Ich kann das bloß nicht aushalten.

*Auch wenn die Effekte also mit Berechnung erzeugt sind, möchten
Sie nicht den Eindruck einer wohlkomponierten visuellen Darstellung
erwecken?*

Nein, im Gegenteil, ich möchte Unmittelbarkeit erreichen –
das Gefühl, als sei das Bild in einem einzigen Augenblick gemalt
worden. Mir gefällt es auch, mit den größten Pinseln zu arbeiten,
die ich einsetzen kann, die innerhalb der Form verwendbar sind.
Ich möchte den Eindruck erzeugen, irgendein Riese hätte etwas
plump seine Hand ausgestreckt und so dieses Zufallsprodukt erzeugt; es darf auch gerne etwas größer sein.

*Sie haben sich konsequenterweise entschieden, Ihre Objekte in
einem nicht-figurativen Raum abzubilden. Was geschieht mit Ihren
Motiven, wenn Sie sie auf diese Weise de-kontextualisieren?*

Ich finde, das drückt mein Interesse am Skulpturalen aus –
daran, eine Form wiederzugeben –, und außerdem meine ich
auch, dass es den Motiven dient, wenn ich darauf verzichte, sie
in einem Raum zu positionieren. Es hebt ihre Körperlichkeit und
ihre eigene Räumlichkeit hervor, denn so gut wie alle meine Motive tragen Räumlichkeit in sich. Es sind Gegenstände, die etwas
enthalten können – eine Vase, ein Zelt, einen Schuh –, und darum
wollte ich nicht, dass um sie herum ein Raum erscheint.

*Aber obwohl Sie leicht wiedererkennbare Formen aussuchen, ver-
mittelt Ihre Wahl der Größe und der Farben das Gefühl von Motiven,
die im Sinne Claes Oldenburgs „larger than life" sind …*

Wenn man ein Motiv wie diesen Schuh hier (*Sko*, 2006; Abb.
S. 15) zu einer solchen Größe, wie er sie hier bekommen hat, auf-
bläst, also auf 2 × 2 Meter, dann verändert sich das Ding natürlich
und wird zu etwas anderem und zu mehr als einem einfachen Objekt. Der Raum im Innern des Schuhs gewinnt Transzendenz über
die Form des Schuhs hinaus und wird nahezu selber eine Form
von Körper oder eigenständig physisch greifbarem Raum. Wenn
man Dinge vergrößert, entsteht eine neue Situation, in der der
Körper sich notwendigerweise neu orientieren muss. Und eben
diese Reorientierung ist interessant.

Und das ist überhaupt etwas, was mich an Form und Figuration interessiert: Dass man ständig versucht, vorgegebene Begriffe zu erweitern und Vorstellungen, die man von den Dingen
hat, an einen ganz anderen Ort zu verschieben, sodass man ge-
zwungen ist, beim Anblick des Bildes zu zweifeln und nachzuspüren. Es lässt sich nichts Selbstverständliches ableiten, man
kann nicht einfach sagen: „Das da ist ein Schuh", denn das ergibt
keinen Sinn. Es erinnert mehr schlecht als recht an einen Schuh,
trotzdem erkennt man die Struktur; wenn es also kein Schuh ist,
was ist es dann? Und das ist genau das, was ich mit einem Bild
auslösen will, dieses „… aber was ist es dann?" In letzter Konse-
quenz bringt einen das nämlich dahin, dass man sich nicht nur
fragt, was ein Schuh ist, sondern – viel bedeutender: Was ist eigentlich ein Gemälde?

Ich versuche, meine Objekte zweideutig erscheinen zu lassen,
denn ich kann es nicht ausstehen, wenn ich ein Bild zu leicht
entschlüsseln kann. Das ist auch der Grund dafür, dass ich mich
so furchtbar schwertue mit Botschaften und mit allzu ausgeprägt
kommunizierender Kunst. Es gibt viele andere Medien, mit denen
Konklusionen und Analysen erheblich besser vermittelt werden
können. Ich denke nicht, dass das die stärkste Seite von Kunst ist.
Für mich ist es viel interessanter, möglichst eine gewisse Zwei-
deutigkeit, Sinnlichkeit oder Neugier zu bewahren: Das ist es, was
ich in meinen Arbeiten versuche. Das Gefühl zu erzeugen: Das
hier ist unmöglich oder dumm oder albern, aber es soll gleichzeitig toll oder hübsch sein. Diese Spannung zwischen Gegensätzen
soll möglichst immer gegenwärtig sein.

*In der Einführung zur Ausstellung steht, dass die Dinge bei Ihnen
eine ganz spezielle „Buch-Form" erhalten. Wie würden Sie diese Form
beschreiben?*

Wenn ich mich so umschaue, scheint es eine ziemlich plumpe
Form zu sein, nicht wahr? Das hängt wahrscheinlich damit zusammen, dass ich gerne schöne Farben verwende; da brauche ich
die Plumpheit und das Grobe als Gegengewicht. Und das betrifft
nicht nur so etwas Oberflächliches wie die Farben. Auf inhaltlicher
Ebene handelt es sich um einen Protest gegen den Körper. Gerne
schaffe ich die eine oder andere Unmöglichkeit: Einen Körper, der
nicht gehorcht, ein Gefühl im Bild, dass etwas schiefgeht oder un-
genau ist und entgleist. Aber gleichzeitig soll eine durchgehende
Schärfe und Klarheit präsent sein, man fühlt einen klaren Kopf
und einen ungehorsamen Körper. So würde ich eigentlich gerne
malen: Es gibt einen Raum, in dem ein Kurzschluss aller Ideen
stattfindet, und alle Dinge verlieren ihre handgreifliche Substanz.
Tatsächlich aber bezieht sich die Buch-Form wohl auf irgendeine
Art Plumpheit, die es erschwert, an einer eindeutigen Begriffswelt
festzuhalten. Die Begriffe fallen ein bisschen auseinander, weil die
Dinge nicht ganz so wollen, wie sie normalerweise wollen.

*Weil die Form plump wird?*

Weil der Körper plump ist, und vielleicht ist er nicht so, wie
wir denken, dass er ist, vielleicht nicht einmal so, wie wir ihn beschreiben. Ich glaube, das will diese Form ausdrücken, dass unsere Vorstellungen herausgefordert werden.

Das Gespräch wurde erstmals in der Online-Ausgabe der Internetzeitschrift *www.Kopenhagen.dk* in dänischer Sprache veröffent-
licht. Die Übertragung ins Englische besorgte Morten Visby; die
englische Übersetzung redigierte Marisia Kucharski. Christine
von Bülow übersetzte die Vorlage ins Deutsche.

*So even if the various effects are deliberate, you are not trying to convey the impression of a carefully constructed visual representation?*

No, on the contrary, I want to achieve a sense of immediacy, as though the painting has been painted in an instant. I also like to use as large a brush possible, as large as is practical given the form. I try to create the impression that some giant could have clumsily reached out his hand and quite randomly created something; even bigger would also be fine.

*You have quite consistently chosen to depict your objects in a non-figurative – or abstract – space. What does this kind of de-contextualisation do to your motifs?*

I think it conveys my interest in the sculptural – in the rendering of a form. Furthermore, I believe that the motifs benefit from my refusal to locate them in space. It emphasises their physical and intrinsically spatial nature; after all pretty much all of my motifs possess an inherent spatiality. They are objects that can contain something, a vase, a tent a shoe, which is why I did not want them to be surrounded by a space.

*But although you choose to work with easily recognisable forms, your choice of size and colour conveys the impression of a motif that, in a Claes Oldenburg sense, becomes 'larger than life' …*

When you blow up a motif, like this shoe for instance (*Sko*, 2006; ill. p. 15), to the proportions you see here, that is to say 2 × 2 metres, then of course the thing will undergo a change and become something else, something more than an ordinary object. The space inside the shoe transcends the form of the shoe and virtually becomes a form of body itself or an independent and physically tangible space. Magnifying things creates a new situation in which the body is forced to re-adjust and it is this readjustment or re-orientation that is interesting.

This is something that really interests me about form and figuration: the continual attempt to expand given concepts and to unseat preconceived images of things, so that, looking at the painting, we are compelled to question it and to explore deeper. You cannot draw any obvious conclusions, you cannot simply say, "This here is a shoe", because there is nothing meaningful conveyed by that. Despite bearing only the tiniest resemblance to a shoe, the structure is still recognisable; so if it is not a shoe, what is it? And this is precisely what I want my paintings to do, to trigger this "… but, what is it then?" Ultimately, you see, this leads you to question, not only what a shoe is, but – more importantly – to question the very essence of what a painting is.

I try to make the objects ambiguous, because I hate it when it is too easy to decode a painting. This is also why I find it so hard to deal with direct messages and art that is overly communicative. Many other media are considerably better suited to the mediation of conclusions and analyses. As I see it, this is not art's strong point. I find it much more interesting to attempt to maintain a certain ambiguity, receptiveness or curiosity, and this is what I attempt to achieve with my work. To create a feeling that something is impossible or stupid or silly, and yet at the same time it should be impressive or beautiful. As far as possible, this tension between opposites should always be present.

*According to the introductory material accompanying the exhibition, in the course of your work things acquire a very unique 'Buch form'. How would you describe this form?*

When I take a look around me, it appears to be quite an awkward form, doesn't it? This may have something to do with the fact that I am so fond of painting with bright colours and so I need the awkwardness and the rawness to act as a counterweight. But it runs deeper than a mere question of colour. On a more thematic level, it is also a protest against the body. I like to create some sort of impossibility: a body that does not do what it is told, a sense, within the painting itself, that something is going wrong, is unclear and going off the rails. But at the same time, there should be a persistent definition or clarity about it, the impression of a clear mind within a non-compliant body. This is the way I would really like to paint: a space in which all ideas are short-circuited and where everything becomes intangible. Maybe the 'Buch form' is really about some kind of awkwardness that makes it difficult to adhere to a clear-cut set of concepts. The concepts begin to disintegrate a little, because things won't quite behave the way they normally do.

*Because the form becomes awkward?*

Because the body is awkward and because maybe it is not the way we imagine it to be, maybe not even the way we describe it. I believe that this is what this form is all about – challenging our concepts.

The interview was first published in Danish in the internet based magazine *www.Kopenhagen.dk*. The translation into English was provided by Morten Visby and revised by Marisia Kucharski. The original Danish material was translated into German by Christine von Bülow.

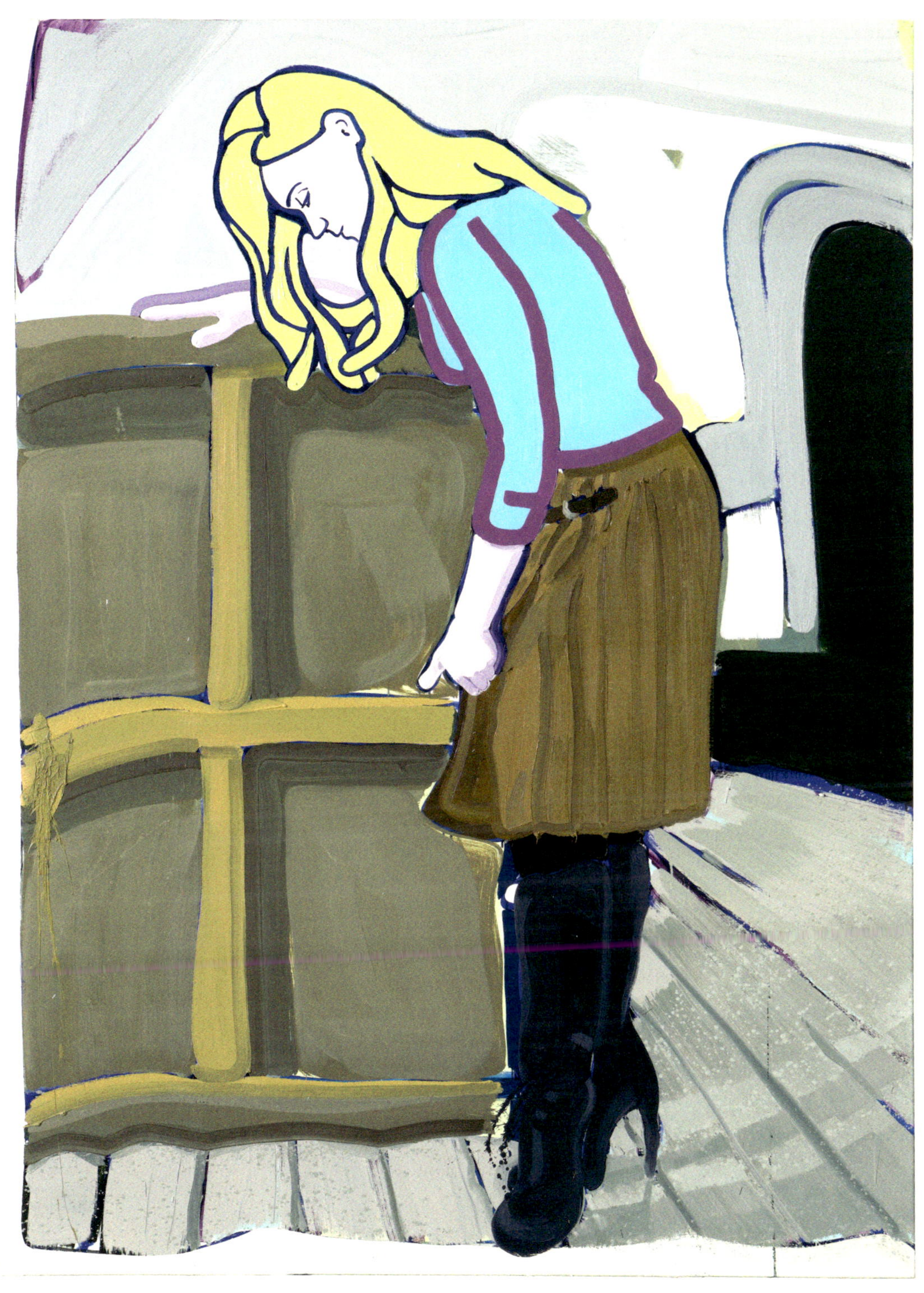

**Lotte** 2007

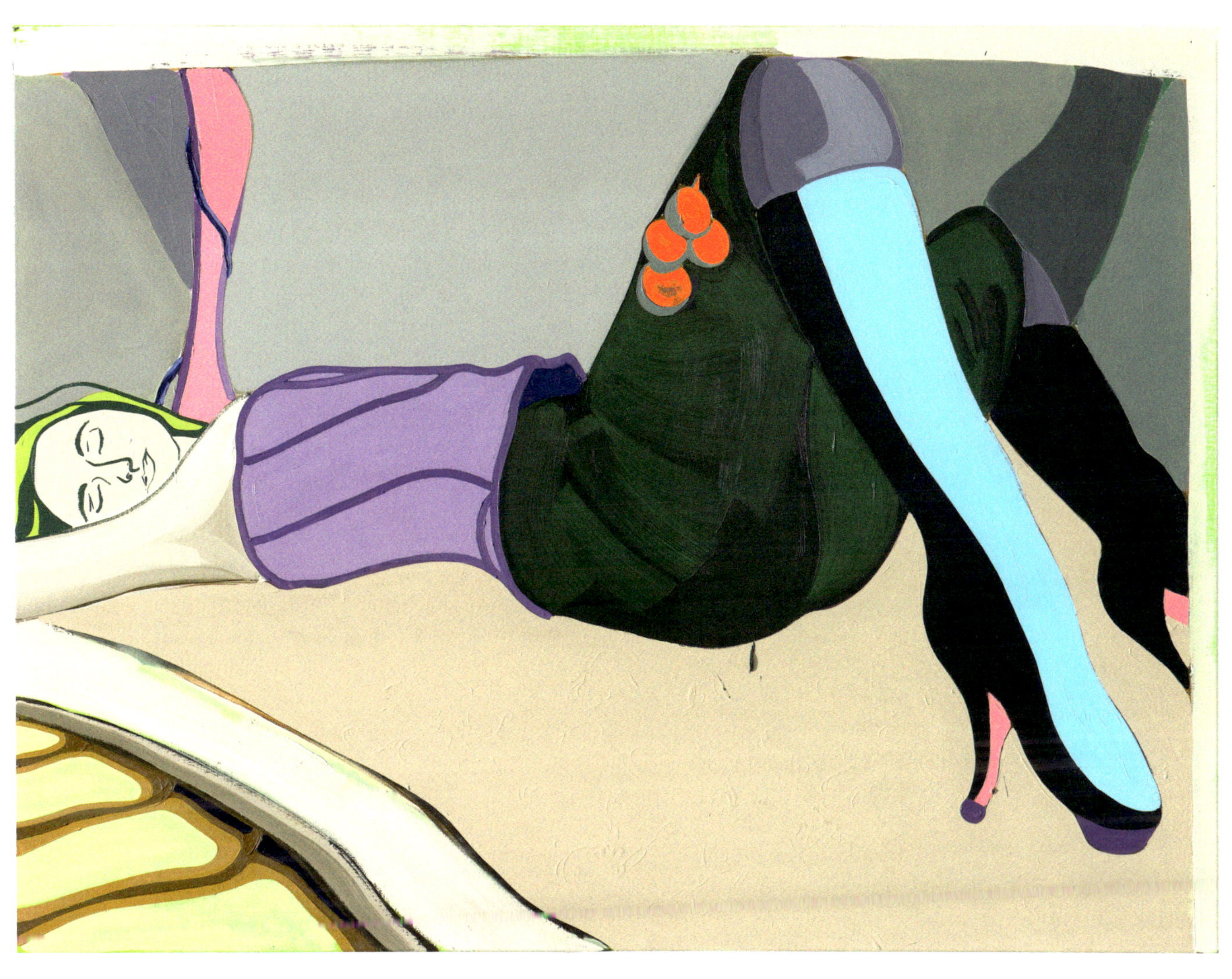

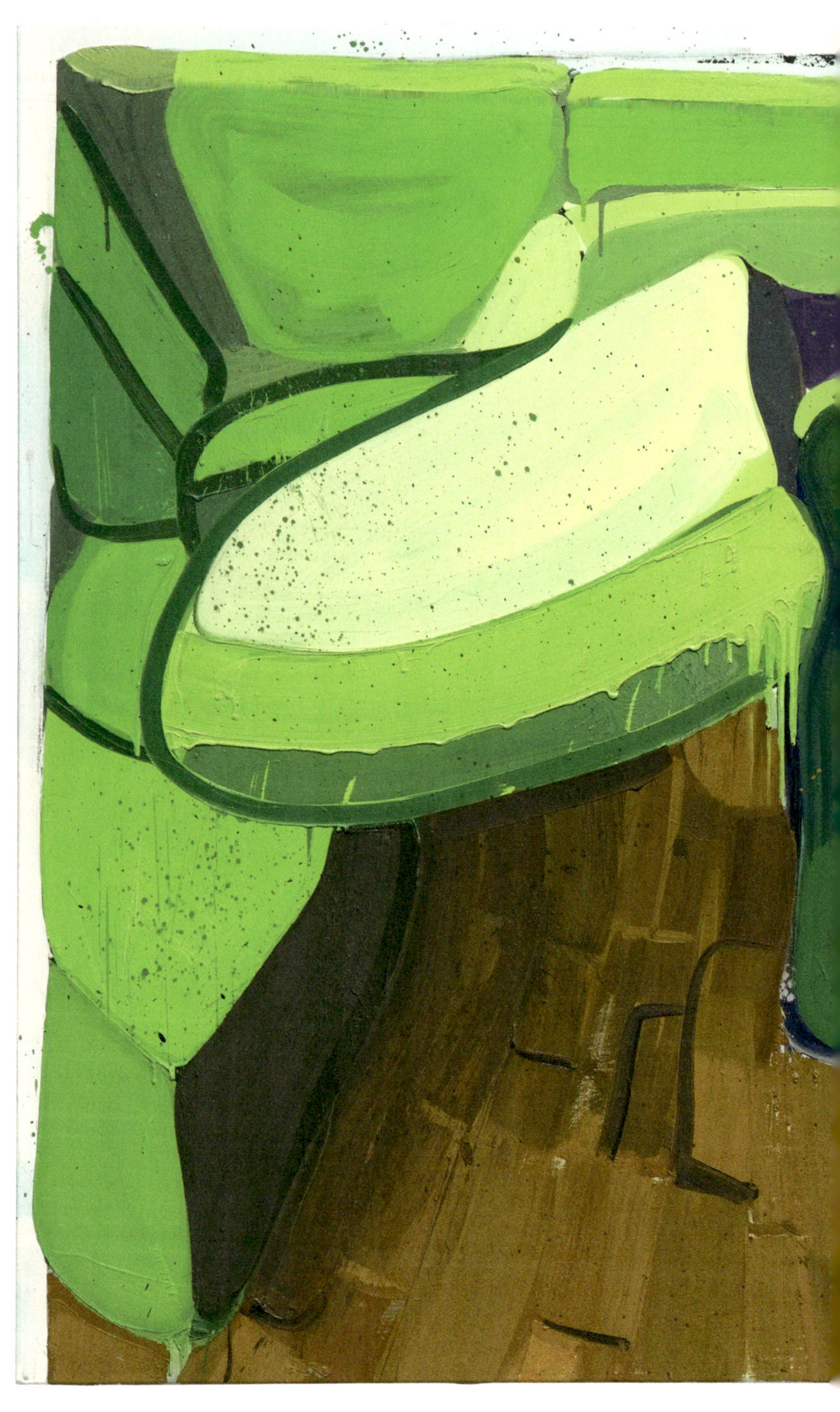

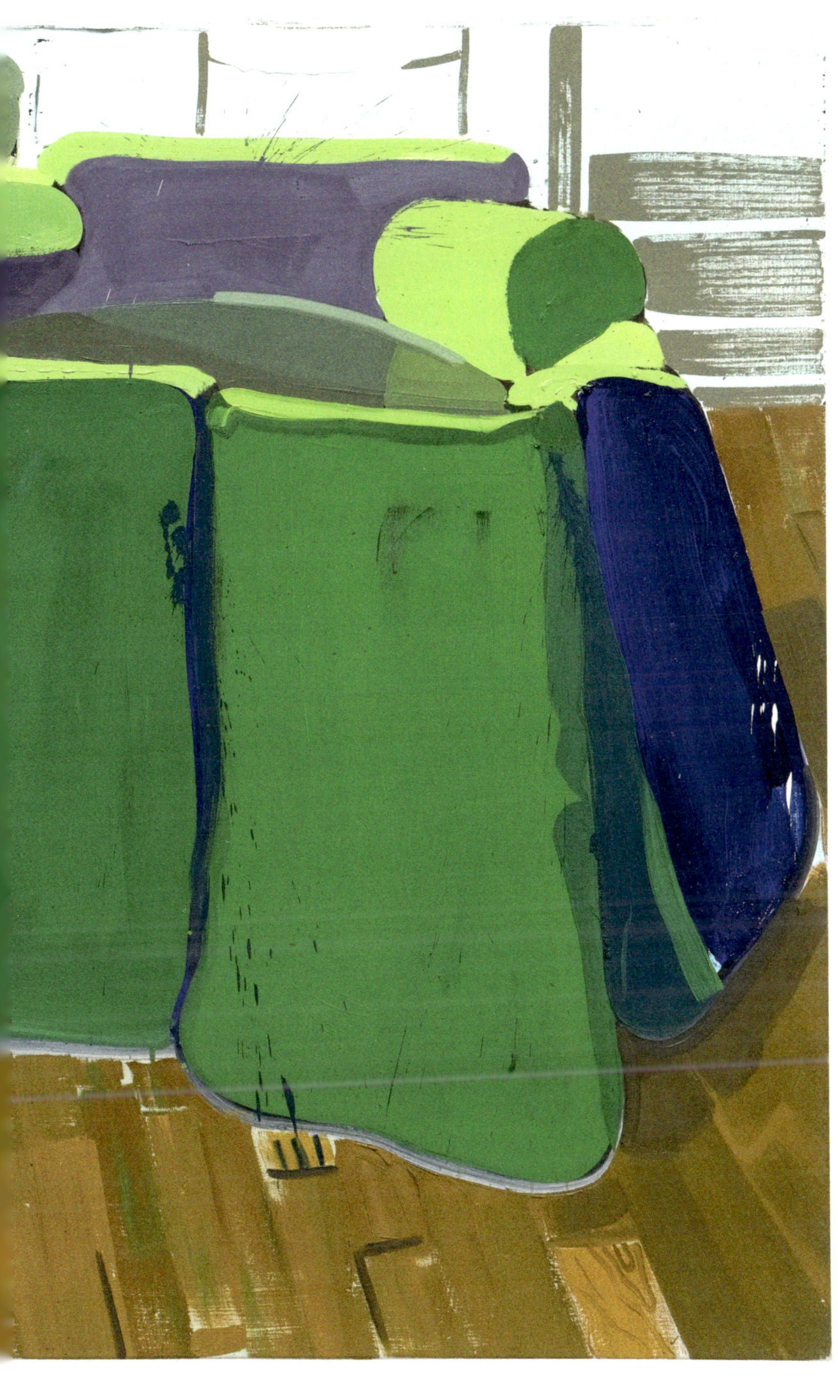

Sofa 2007

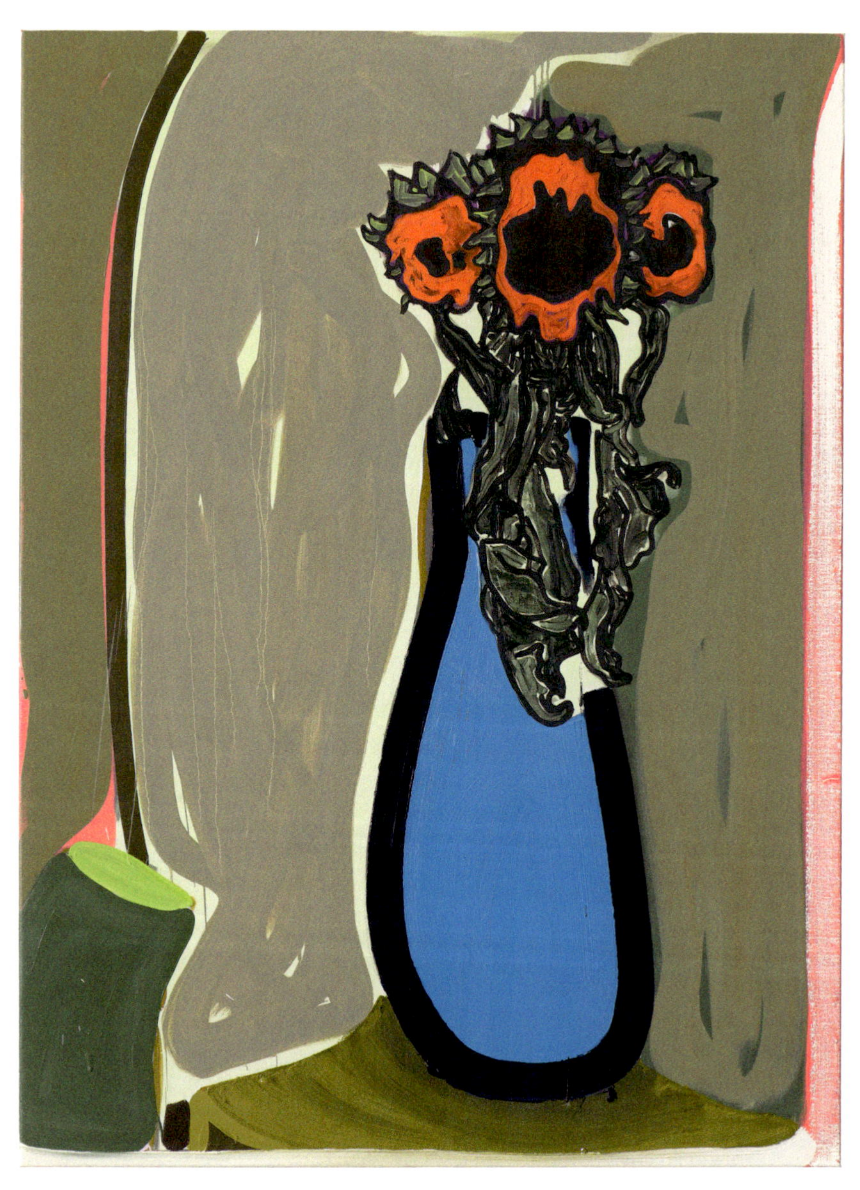



**Vase** 2008

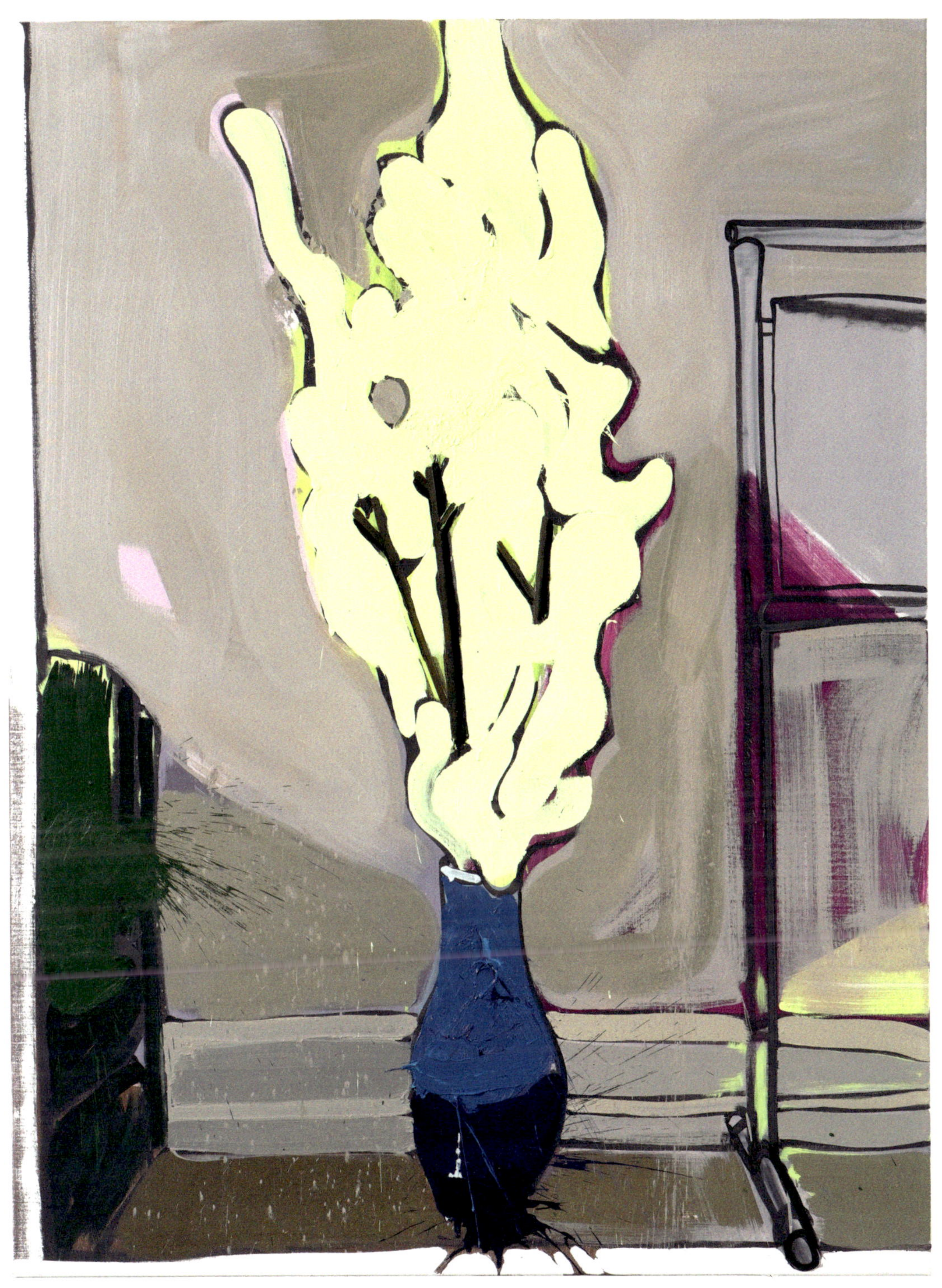

**Vase** 2006

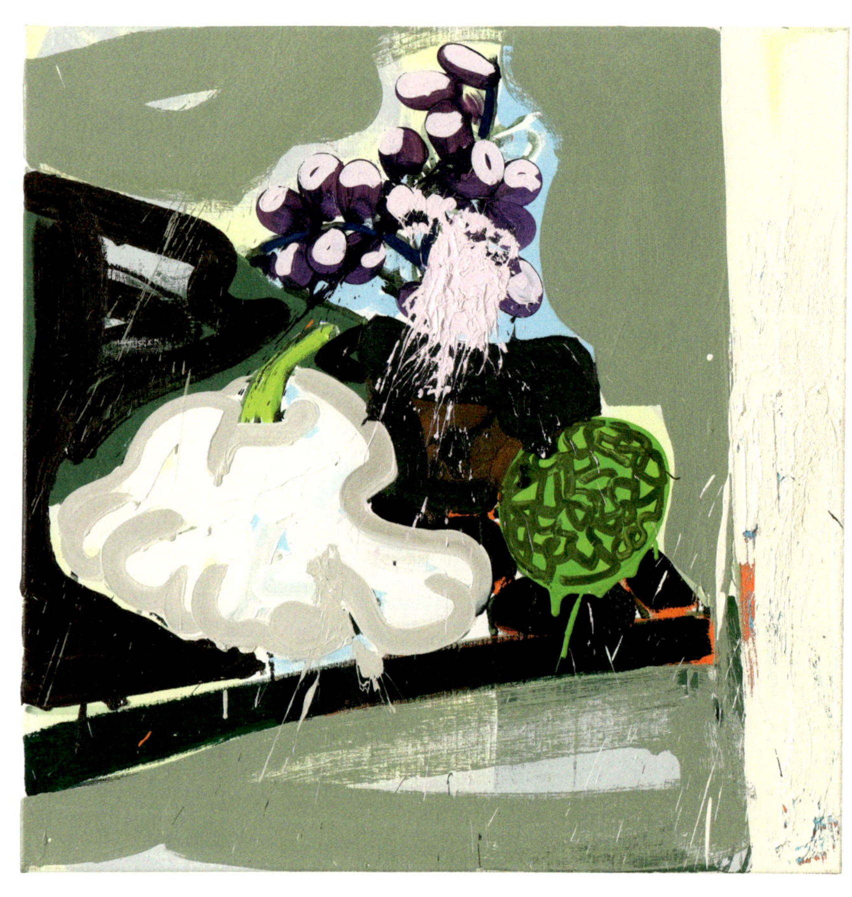



**Opstilling** 2007

# Biografie | Biography

**Morten Buch**
Geboren in Kopenhagen 1970, lebt und arbeitet in Kopenhagen | Born 1970 in Copenhagen, lives and works in Copenhagen. Autodidakt | Autodidact

**Einzelausstellungen | Solo Exhibitions**

2006    *No Halo,* Galleri Susanne Ottesen, København
2005    *One,* Galerie MøllerWitt, Århus
2004    *mellemrum,* Galleri Susanne Ottesen, København
2003    Galerie MøllerWitt, Århus
Galerie Renate Schröder, Köln
*everything's alright,* DCA Gallery, New York, USA, mit | with Jasper Sebastian Stürup
2001    *This here – That there,* Galleri Susanne Ottesen, København
2000    *Zero Hour I–VI* mit | with Jacob Leth Jensen, Galleri Susanne Ottesen, København
1997    *Éclairs I–VIII* mit | with Jacob Leth Jensen, Galleri Susanne Ottesen, København

**Ausgewählte Gruppenausstellungen**
**Selected Group Exhibitions**

2008    *InnenRaum,* Galerie MøllerWitt, Århus
2007    *real inside – unreal outside,* Galleri Susanne Ottesen, København
Grønningen, Kunsthal Charlottenborg, København
*Show Off III,* Galerie MøllerWitt, Århus
2006    *Malerhjerne,* Arken Museum of Modern Art, Ishøj/København
2003    *Accrochage,* Galleri Susanne Ottesen, København
2002    *Skulptur Maleri Tegning* mit | with Martin Erik Andersen und | and Jasper Sebastian Stürup, Galleri Susanne Ottesen, København
2001    *Museumssammlung | Museum Collection,* Arken Museum of Modern Art, Ishøj/København
2000    *Accrochage,* Galleri Susanne Ottesen, København
*Take-off 20:01,* Aarhus Kunstmuseum, Århus

**Preise und Stipendien**
**Awards and Scholarships**

2007    The Danish Arts Foundation's Working Grant
2006    The Danish Arts Foundation's Working Grant
2002/03   The Danish Art Foundation's Two-Year Working Scholarship
1996    Marie Langhoff Grant, København

**Im Besitz öffentlicher Sammlungen**
**Public Collections**

Horsens Kunstmuseum, Horsens
Arken Museum of Modern Art, Ishøj/ København
Statens Kunstfond, København

*Dobbeltmadras | Doppelmatratze | Double-mattress*, 2006
Öl auf Leinwand | Oil on canvas,
200 × 200 cm
Danish Arts Council
Abb. S. | ill. p. 27

*Dobbeltmadras | Doppelmatratze | Double-mattress*, 2006
Öl auf Leinwand | Oil on canvas,
200 × 200 cm
Private collection
Abb. S. | ill. p. 29

*Pibe | Pfeife | Pipe*, 2006
Öl auf Leinwand | Oil on canvas,
200 × 200 cm
Private collection
Abb. S. | ill. p. 33

*Pibe | Pfeife | Pipe*, 2006
Öl auf Leinwand | Oil on canvas,
200 × 200 cm
Private collection
Abb. S. | ill. p. 35

*Sko | Schuh | Shoe*, 2006
Öl auf Leinwand | Oil on canvas,
200 × 200 cm
Samling Løvbjerg
Abb. S. | ill. p. 15

*Sko | Schuh | Shoe*, 2006
Öl auf Leinwand | Oil on canvas,
200 × 200 cm
Private collection
Abb. S. | ill. p. 17

*Sko | Schuh | Shoe*, 2006
Öl auf Leinwand | Oil on canvas,
160 × 160 cm
Private collection
Abb. S. | ill. p. 18

*Sko | Schuh | Shoe*, 2006
Öl auf Leinwand | Oil on canvas,
200 × 200 cm
Danish Arts Council
Abb. S. | ill. p. 19

*Stol | Stuhl | Chair*, 2006
Öl auf Leinwand | Oil on canvas,
200 × 200 cm
Private collection
Abb. S. | ill. p. 31

*Stol | Stuhl | Chair*, 2006
Öl auf Leinwand | Oil on canvas,
200 × 200 cm
Private collection
Abb. S. | ill. p. 66

*Telt | Zelt | Tent*, 2006
Öl auf Leinwand | Oil on canvas,
300 × 300 cm
Danish Arts Council
Abb. S. | ill. p. 24/25

*Vase*, 2006
Öl auf Leinwand | Oil on canvas,
200 × 200 cm
Henrik Sindet-Beck
Abb. S. | ill. p. 21

*Vase*, 2006
Öl auf Leinwand | Oil on canvas,
200 × 200 cm
Private collection
Abb. S. | ill. p. 23

*Vase*, 2006
Öl auf Leinwand | Oil on canvas,
200 × 200 cm
Horsens Kunstmuseum
Abb. S. | ill. p. 37

*Vase*, 2006
Öl auf Leinwand | Oil on canvas,
240 × 240 cm
Rasmus & Jane Refer, København
Abb. S. | ill. p. 56/57

*Vase*, 2006
Öl auf Leinwand | Oil on canvas,
200 × 150 cm
Brask Collection
Abb. S. | ill. p. 91

*Landskab | Landschaft | Landscape*, 2007
Öl auf Leinwand | Oil on canvas,
200 × 200 cm
Courtesy Galleri Susanne Ottesen,
København
Abb. S. | ill. p. 69

*Landskab | Landschaft | Landscape*, 2007
Öl auf Leinwand | Oil on canvas,
200 × 200 cm
Private collection
Abb. S. | ill. p. 71

# Check-list of works

*Lotte,* 2007
Öl auf Leinwand | Oil on canvas,
200 × 150 cm
Courtesy Galleri Susanne Ottesen,
København
Abb. S. | ill. p. 85

*Opstilling | Stillleben | Still Life,* 2007
Öl auf Leinwand | Oil on canvas,
90 × 90 cm
Fondazione Aldega, Amelia, Italy
Abb. S. | ill. p. 92

*Sofa,* 2007
Öl auf Leinwand | Oil on canvas,
180 × 240 cm
Horsens Kunstmuseum
Abb. S. | ill. p. 88/89

*Stilleben | Stillleben | Still Life,* 2007
Öl auf Leinwand | Oil on canvas,
200 × 200 cm
Henrik Sindet-Beck
Abb. | ill. p. 76

*Stilleben | Stillleben | Still Life,* 2007
Öl auf Leinwand | Oil on canvas,
200 × 200 cm
Private collection
Abb. | ill. p. 77

*Dobbeltmadras | Doppelmatratze |
Double-mattress,* 2008
Öl auf Leinwand | Oil on canvas,
200 × 200 cm
Courtesy Galleri Susanne Ottesen,
København
Abb. S. | ill. p. 38

*Dobbeltmadras | Doppelmatratze |
Double-mattress,* 2008
Öl auf Leinwand | Oil on canvas,
200 × 200 cm
Courtesy Galleri Susanne Ottesen,
København
Abb. S. | ill. p. 39

*Landskab | Landschaft | Landscape,* 2008
Öl auf Leinwand | Oil on canvas,
270 × 360 cm
Courtesy Galleri Susanne Ottesen,
København
Abb. | ill. p. 72/73

*Lotte,* 2008
Öl auf Leinwand | Oil on canvas,
150 × 200 cm
Courtesy Galleri Susanne Ottesen,
København
Abb. S. | ill. p. 87

*Sko | Schuh | Shoe,* 2008
Öl auf Leinwand | Oil on canvas,
300 × 300 cm
Courtesy Galleri Susanne Ottesen,
København
Abb. S. | ill. p. 40/41

*Stilleben | Stillleben | Still Life,* 2008
Öl auf Leinwand | Oil on canvas,
240 × 240 cm
Courtesy Galleri Susanne Ottesen,
København
Abb. S. | ill. p. 75

*Uden Titel | Ohne Titel | Untitled,* 2008
Öl auf Leinwand | Oil on canvas,
90 × 90 cm
Courtesy Galleri Susanne Ottesen,
København
Abb. S. | ill. p. 79

*Vase,* 2008
Öl auf Leinwand | Oil on canvas,
160 × 120 cm
Samling Løvbjerg
Abb. S. | ill. p. 90

*Vase,* 2008
Öl auf Leinwand | Oil on canvas,
200 × 200 cm
Courtesy Galleri Susanne Ottesen,
København
Abb. S. | ill. p. 67

Diese Publikation erscheint anlässlich der Ausstellung | The catalogue is published on the occasion of the exhibition
*Morten Buch – The Last Resort | Letzte Zuflucht*
Kunsthalle Wilhelmshaven, 4.7. – 14.9.2008
Horsens Kunstmuseum, 4.10. – 7.12.2008

**Ausstellung | Exhibition**
Morten Buch, Viola Weigel

**Kunsthalle Wilhelmshaven**
Leitung | Director
    Viola Weigel
Sekretariat | Administration
    Silvana Bräutigam, Dagmar Hinrichs
Ausstellungstechnik | Technical support
    Wolfgang Conrads

Kunsthalle Wilhelmshaven
Adalbertstraße 28
D-26382 Wilhelmshaven
Telefon +49(0)4421 41448
Telefax +49(0)4421 43987
www.kunsthalle-wilhelmshaven.de
kunsthalle.wilhelmshaven@t-online.de

**Horsens Kunstmuseum**
Carolinelundsvej 2
DK-8700 Horsens
Telefon +45(0)76 292370
www.horsenskunstmuseum.dk
kunstmuseum@horsens.dk

**Katalog | Catalogue**
Herausgeberin | Editor
    Viola Weigel
Katalog | Catalogue
    Viola Weigel, Morten Buch
Texte | Texts
    Viola Weigel, Claus Hagedorn-Olsen,
    Maibritt Pedersen

Redaktion | Edited by
    Viola Weigel
Lektorat | Copy-editing, proofreading
    Sophie Reinhardt, Viola Weigel
Übersetzung | Translations
    Dänisch – Deutsch | Danish – German:
    Christine von Bülow, Kiel; Dänisch –
    Englisch | Danish – English: Morten
    Visby, Kopenhagen; Deutsch – Eng-
    lisch | German – English: Marisia
    Kucharski, Aberdeen
Fotografie | Photography
    Anders Sune Berg (Morten Buch);
    Städel Museum/Artothek (Juncker,
    Liebermann); Klaus-Martin Treder
    (Recom GmbH, Ostfildern); Felix
    Tirry (Luc Tuymans)
Bildbearbeitung | Picture editing
    Anders Sune Berg
Gestaltung | Design
    Andreas Koch
Gesamtherstellung | Printed and
published by
    Kerber Verlag, Bielefeld
    Windelsbleicher Straße 166 – 170
    33659 Bielefeld
    Germany
    Telefon +49(0)521 9 50 08-10
    Telefax +49(0)521 9 50 08-88
    www.kerberverlag.com
    info@kerberverlag.com
Kerber, US Distribution
    D.A.P., Distributed Art Publishers Inc.
    155 Sixth Avenue 2nd Floor
    New York, N.Y. 10013
    phone +1(0)212 6 27-19 99
    fax +1(0)212 6 27-94 84
Umschlag vorn | Cover
    MORTEN BUCH, *Vase*, 2006, Öl auf Lein-
    wand | Oil on canvas, 200 × 200 cm,
    Henrik Sindet-Beck

S. | p. 2/3, 12/13: Ausstellung | Exhibition
    *Morten Buch – No Halo*, 2006, Galleri
    Susanne Ottesen, København
S. | p. 6: Morten Buchs Atelier | Morten
    Buch's atelier, København 2008
S. | p. 64/65: Ausstellung | Exhibition
    *Grønningen*, 2007, Kunsthal Charlotten-
    borg, København


Die Deutsche Nationalbibliothek verzeich-net diese Publikation in der Deutschen Nationalbibliografie; detaillierte bibliogra-fische Daten sind im Internet über http://dnb.ddb.de abrufbar. | The Deutsche Biblio-thek holds a record of this publication in the Deutsche Nationalbibliografie; detailed bibliographical data can be found under: http://dnb.ddb.de



ISBN 978-3-86678-146-7

Printed in Germany

Ausstellung und Katalog werden gefördert von |
Exhibition and catalogue sponsored by

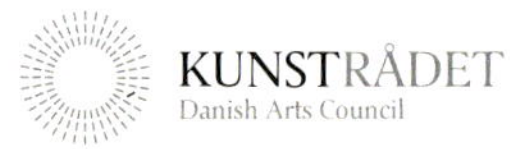
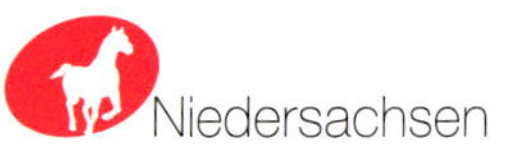
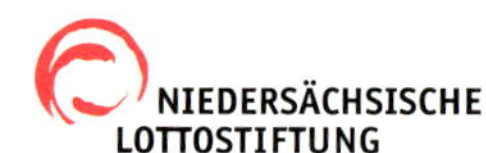
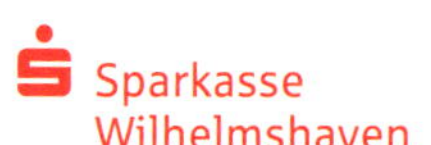
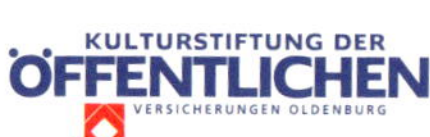